Nonverbal communication

THE BOBBS-MERRILL SERIES IN *Speech Communication*

RUSSEL R. WINDES, *Editor*

ABNE M. EISENBERG
AND
RALPH R. SMITH, JR.

Nonverbal communication

The Bobbs-Merrill Company, Inc.
INDIANAPOLIS AND NEW YORK

Copyright © 1971 by The Bobbs-Merrill Company, Inc.
Printed in the United States of America
Library of Congress Catalog Card Number 77–160790

ISBN-0-672-61155-4

Second Printing

Editor's foreword

The study of speech communication has always been and continues to be almost entirely concerned with **speech.** Theories of rhetoric or communication attempt to analyze sender-receiver and message variables by concentrating mainly on the **verbal** aspects of a single message. As a result, students of speech communication miss the full dramatic experience of interpersonal communication.

Professors Smith and Eisenberg, in **Nonverbal Communication,** attempt to give the student an appreciation of the many-faceted reality of speech communication. They believe that the study of communication should by no means be confined to meaningful interactional events which are **verbal.** Many messages are simultaneously sent during the course of an interaction. Most of these messages are conveyed through nonverbal forms—gestures, bodily movement, spacing, voice, and the environmental setting in which any interaction occurs.

"To study communication," Eisenberg and Smith write, "is to examine all the ways in which human beings send information and integrate their actions and feelings." Speech is not necessarily the most common message form: "In fact, verbal messages may carry far less impact than other message forms." And an analysis of interpersonal communication is incomplete "without a consideration of more than just language use."

Nonverbal Communication is a volume in the Bobbs-Merrill Series in Speech Communication which attempts to complement a word-centered approach to the study of speech communication and apply a multidimensional method to the study of all interpersonal communication events. Professors Smith and Eisenberg seek to motivate the reader "to think differently and more effectively about your own behavior, as well as the behavior of others." We must learn "to think through what our actions say, to achieve flexibility in coping with a broad gamut of people under many different circumstances." Action communication is the complementary channel to verbal communication; unless one understands and relates to both channels, one's perception and comprehension of any communication encounter is distorted.

Scholars in many disciplines have for some time been involved in the exploration of nonverbal communicative behavior. Psychologists have given much attention to kinesics (facial and bodily expression). Social psychologists of the symbolic-interactionist school have theorized extensively about the role of nonverbal communication in sustaining social encounters. Anthropologists have engaged in the study of similarity and difference in nonverbal communication across cultural boundaries in an attempt to determine universal behavior, to analyze separate cultures, and to facilitate cross-cultural communication. Scholars in speech communication have been concerned with those nonverbal expressions which contribute to the effect of a verbal message. In small group communication, research has related to the physical arrangement of participants as a variable in cohesion and sociometric categorization. Throughout academic disciplines, the study of nonverbal communication as an indicator of the real character and personality of both communicator and receiver (and their phenomenological systems) has been growing in popularity and importance.

One of the essential reasons the literature on nonverbal communication has failed to have enormous impact on the speech communication discipline is that heretofore this ample literature was scattered among the journals and writings of many disciplines and therefore was not readily accessible to the student and instructor. Nor is the literature, once found, always in a form which is easily understood. Up to now, two kinds of literature relating to nonverbal communication have been on the market: (1) textbooks on communication which include short treatments of the subject; (2) specialized monographs on nonverbal communication covering a limited area in great depth.

Professors Eisenberg and Smith have attempted to provide for the student of speech communication the first general treatment of the literature of nonverbal communication. They have collected a cohesive body of materials appropriate to most courses in the discipline and structured these materials into easily readable and understandable essays covering the major issues and topics related to the study of nonverbal communication. **Nonverbal Communication** is not intended to be an all-inclusive review of research in the field. Rather, the book proposes and elaborates a framework within which the interested reader can become knowledgeable about nonverbal communication; he can then pursue particular topics with the aid of both the bibliography and the exercises.

A first work in any field is exceedingly difficult to write, for there are no models to follow. Professors Smith and Eisenberg have worked comfortably amid the difficulties. We believe that the end result, **Nonverbal Communication,** is an important contribution to the speech-communication discipline.

Russel R. Windes

Preface

We first thought of writing a book on nonverbal communication during a series of discussions between us in the winter and spring of 1969. We were both struck with the interest shown by our students in the idea of communication without words. At first our intent was to discover and organize some of the available literature on the subject for classroom presentation, but as we became more deeply involved in our project, the temptation to share our work with a larger audience became stronger. We have yielded to temptation.

The contributions of others to this book clearly stand out in our memory. Professor Joseph DeVito carefully read and commented upon a draft of this work. Professor Russel Windes worked closely with us during each stage of the preparation of the manuscript. We are also indebted to Pearl Eisenberg for her valuable comments on each successive version of our project, and to Dennis Ougourlian for his recommendations in connection with textual illustrations. Last, Professor Eisenberg would like to thank Eric and Danya for lending out their father to this task.

Abne M. Eisenberg
Ralph R. Smith, Jr.

December, 1970

Contents

1. **An introduction to nonverbal communication**   *3*

2. **Definitions, classifications, and problems**   *11*
   Definition of communication, 12
   Definition of nonverbal communication, 20
   Types of nonverbal communication, 22
      Paralanguage, 23
      Kinesics, 27
      Proxemics, 28
   Issues in defining nonverbal communication, 29

3. **Nonverbal meaning: a behavioral approach**   *33*
   Symbols and signs, 34
   Judgment of vocal expression, 35
   Judgment of facial expression, 36
   Origins of nonverbal signs: nature or nurture?, 40
   Summary, 46

4. *Nonverbal meaning: a physiological approach*   **47**

    The body as medium, 47

    The physiology of stimulus reception, 51

    Mental processes and nonverbal communication, 54

    Discrimination, 56

    Regrouping, 57

    Symbol decoding, 57

    Life orientation, ideation, and incubation, 58

    Symbol encoding and transmission, 59

    Summary, 60

5. *Social functions of nonverbal communication*   **62**

    Transmission of information, 62

    Integration of action and feelings, 64

    Communication and social identity, 66

    Self-protection through self-control, 68

    Nonverbal self-presentation and motor coordination, 72

    Summary, 73

6. *Culture and nonverbal meaning:*
    cross-cultural studies   **75**

    Nonverbal ethnocentrism, 75

    Comparison of nonverbal systems, 77

    Comparison of postural communication, 78

    Comparison of movement communication, 80

    Comparison of proxemic communication, 85

    Culture, personality, and expression, 88

    Ethnicity and tolerance, 89

    Summary, 90

7. *Culture and nonverbal meaning: a study in*
    American behavioral patterns   **92**

    Eye movement, 92

    Facial expression, 95

Posture, 98
Movement as gesture, 99
Distance, 101
Personal appearance and clothing, 105
Summary, 107

8. *Exercises in nonverbal communication*   *108*
Stereophonic speaking, 109
What's in a name?, 110
Nonverbal autobiography, 111
Dialogue in darkness, 112
Acoustic dampening, 113
Open net/closed net, 114
Touch and tell, 115
Proxemics and the small group, 116
Nonverbal communication through smell, 118
International taste festival, 119
Proxemics: sociopedality on a one-to-one basis, 120

Bibliography, 123

Index, 129

Nonverbal communication

ONE

An introduction to nonverbal communication

A common denominator binds together all who will profit from reading this book: a concern for understanding the communication of thoughts and emotions among men. This concern may be prompted by a superficial need to study communication, or it may be inspired by an abiding curiosity about human behavior. Moreover, the reader of this book may merely wish to become a more popular, persuasive person. However, we hope that self-centered objectives, when realized, will lead to an altruistic desire to see all men improve the quality of their lives through open and meaningful communication.

We require many kinds of information to achieve a knowledge of human behavior. Some kinds can only be gathered through experience and self-analysis, but much of the rest is acquired more formally, through the study of literature, history, comparative cultures, and social psychology. The study of man's accumulated store of information and interpretation, and the introspective study of oneself, are necessary complements to each other. If self-analysis does not draw upon the thoughts of other minds, it is idiosyncratic and circular. Without introspection, however, the study of human behavior is mechanical and barren.

Until recent years, the study of communication has been marked

3

by a disparity between formal and experiential knowledge. A lifetime of relating to people has taught us that there are many ways to get inside another's head, to discern and understand the ideas and emotions of those with whom we seek contact. The formal study of communication, however, has traditionally emphasized the use of language to the exclusion of all other forms of communication. And since a formal knowledge of communication is acquired by taking courses in writing and speaking, problems in communication have been largely regarded as misunderstandings in the use of words— semantic breakdowns. This preoccupation with words has percolated into the public mind. We express the concept of interaction with another by phrases that emphasize verbal behavior, such as, "We talked." Your own experience will tell you, however, that more than a mere exchange of words occurs when people enter one another's presence. There is a physical approach—smiles, frowns, blinks, gestures, and sighs. All these actions convey meaning, but in the context of a word-centered study of communication, they would be considered unimportant.

The premise of this book is that analysis of interpersonal communication is incomplete without a consideration of more than mere use of language. If you were to write down your next conversation, would that transcription fully capture the sense and feeling of what happened? Obviously not. The crucial messages which were unspoken would be missing—the reassuring smile, the trembling hand, the looks of concern, anger, or derision. A skilled actor creates the "business" which turns words in a script into a believable portrayal of human behavior. While one actor is speaking, gesticulating, grimacing, and posturing, his fellow players are reacting to him, to the physical setting on the stage, and to the audience, and are becoming involved in peripheral actions. If the actors failed to do more than merely recite the words in the script, they would create an impression of artificiality because real communication consists of a continuous flow of many different kinds of action which are meaningful to the people involved in the communication. The study of communication, like the mastering of acting, demands careful attention to both the use of language and all other ways by which human beings convey meaning.

To communicate something, you do not have to say explicitly what you mean. In fact, a basic strategem in communication is to say what you believe the other person wants to hear while simultaneously indicating insincerity through a physical action. Do any of the following snippets of dialogue seem familiar?

Exchange #1

Person **A**: That's right, isn't it?   [With an intense look that changes the question mark into an exclamation point.]

Person **B**: I believe that's correct.   [With a look of intimidated disbelief.]

Exchange #2

Person **A**: Do you love me?   [Inching nearer, with a look indicating that **A** will become hostile if the wrong answer is given.]

Person **B**: Deeply.   [Inching quickly away.]

Exchange #3

Person **A**: Hello.   [Cheerfully, with a look of pleasure.]

Person **B**: Glad to see you.   [With grimace, eyes to the ground, shoulders slumped.]

In each of these exchanges, person **B**'s actions contradict his verbal statement (pseudo-affective behavior). **The meaning of each communication is to be found neither in words spoken, nor in the actions, but in both, understood in relationship to one another.**

All these examples can be analyzed in the same way: person **A** demands by word and manner a favorable response and, under duress, **B** supplies the appropriate verbal formula, but is unable or unwilling to mask his feelings completely. Sometimes, as in cases just described, the various ways man can express himself are in jarring dissonance. More commonly, perhaps, words and acts are in harmony. The coordination between what we say and the way in which we act is so precise and automatic that it is not always noticeable, except when an unusual situation arises. Say the word "hello." Did you notice the corners of your lips begin to pull back into a smile? Now smile broadly and say, "I hate you!" The combination should have felt strange because certain expressions and movements do not make sense in conjunction with particular words. Now say, "I hate you!" with a snarl. That makes sense because the act incorporates and thus emphasizes the verbal meaning. In similar ways, actions constantly add to and emphasize the words you speak. Actions can even replace words as the primary carriers of meaning for people who have known one another for a very long time.

Communicative actions do more than clarify, contradict, or replace verbal messages, however. They provide information vital to the conduct of social life. An eminent social psychologist observes that, "To take our place with others we must perceive each other's existence, and reach a measure of comprehension of one another's needs, emotions and thoughts."[1] And part of what we must know about others in order to relate to and comprehend them comes from such simple actions as the way an individual sits, walks, and stands. These behaviors may reveal much about his background, attitudes, and intentions. You might well take a moment now to think back to the strangers whom you have seen in the last few hours. Can you make summary judgments about their occupations, their life styles, and their availability to you as social companions? We assume that with various degrees of accuracy such judgments can be and are constantly being made.

A person's relationship to others is often defined by action. For example, we would not go to our friends shouting, "I am better (or worse) than you." But our behavior can signal our belief that we have a rank on a "status ladder." Who, we notice, presumes to sit at the head of the table? And who insists that his companion go through the door first? These games are important for establishing a position in a group.

One of the most important forms of communication involves neither words nor expressive body movements. Through purposeful action, men arrange the objects in their environment in such a way as to provide a window into their minds. The cluttered desk or the neat one, ragged clothes or clean, hair short or long, kempt or uncombed —these objects are, together with other signs, definitive of their possessors. Think about the ways your friends' rooms and clothes reflect their personalities.

Every functioning member of a society is able to send and interpret many communicative acts. The average individual does not need a book to help interpret a frown or a smile. Therefore, we must ask, why should we bother with formal study of a range of behaviors taught by

[1] S. E. Asch, **Social Psychology** (Englewood Cliffs, N.J.: Prentice-Hall, Inc., 1952), p. 139.

experience, and familiar to all? The Maréchal de Caillière, writing in 1661, forcefully argued that books, like the one you are now reading, serve little purpose:

> The world is a great book which teaches us something every moment, and conversations are living studies which are not a whit inferior to those of books. . . . Habitual conversation with two or three wits can be more useful to us than all the university pedants in the world. . . . They pour out more good sense in one hour than we could read in a library in three days. The movements and the expression of the face have a charm which lends weight to what the tongue has to say.[2]

We do not want you to eschew conversation with wits, or to stop making your own observations about how people behave in one another's presence. Rather, our purpose is the exact opposite. Instead of telling you "everything you always wanted to know about communication, but never thought to ask," our purpose here is to motivate you to try to think differently and more effectively about your own behavior, as well as the behavior of others.

Communicative actions are so familiar to us that most people are insufficiently sensitive to the meaning of their own actions and those of others. A personal style, acquired through years of learning, becomes inflexible, quite beyond control. To take a well-known case, Lyndon Johnson was one of the most successful Senate majority leaders in this nation's history. Among the reasons for his success was his ability to be persuasive in face-to-face encounters. Two journalistic biographers of Johnson, Rowland Evans and Robert Novak, have described "the Johnson treatment," his unique brand of persuasion:

> The treatment could last ten minutes or four hours. It came, enveloping its target . . . wherever Johnson could find a fellow Senator within his reach. Its tone could be supplication, accusation, cajolery, exuberance, scorn, tears, complaint, the hint of threat. It was all of these together. It ran the gamut of human emotion. . . . He moved in close, his face a scant millimeter from his target, his eyes widening and narrowing, his eyebrows rising and falling.[3]

Notice how Evans and Novak emphasize Johnson's actions: the

[2] Quoted in Phillipe Ariès, **Centuries of Childhood: A Social History of Family Life,** trans. Robert Baldick (New York: Random House, Inc., 1962), p. 379.
[3] Rowland Evans and Robert Novak, **Lyndon B. Johnson: The Exercise of Power** (New York: New American Library, 1966), p. 104.

distance from the listener, the tone of voice, the facial expressions. These, as much as his words, constituted Johnson's persuasive appeal. Many other factors account for Johnson's legislative power and for the collapse of his popularity as President. The so-called credibility gap, or his inability to communicate effectively with the American people, is certainly one reason for his unpopularity during the late 1960s. On television he could not stand "a scant millimeter from his target," in order to use the behavioral repertoire which had become fixed by his experience.

Many people have equally rigid methods for dealing with others. Only by making an effort to think through **what actions say** can an individual achieve flexibility in coping with a broad gamut of people under many different circumstances. The following questions might help in thinking about your own communicative patterns:

1. Do you ever avoid talking to someone because he speaks too slowly or too loudly?
2. What are the three most common gestures you make when you speak? Do these gestures say anything about your personality?
3. How do you know that someone is interested in talking with you when that interest is not verbalized?
4. Under what circumstances do you say what you don't mean? When you do, have you ever noticed yourself telling a lie with your face?
5. Why do you act differently when you are in your own house than when you are in the house of a friend?
6. At what distance does a good friend get "too close"? At what distance does a fellow student, whom you do not know well, get "too close"? Why is there a difference?
7. Have you ever felt hostile or friendly toward someone just because of his appearance?
8. Do you sit in the same chair at home? At school? At work? Have you ever gotten angry because someone took **your** seat? Why?

These questions represent only a few of many that can be asked about the way in which you express yourself. One way of thinking through these questions is to review what others have learned about the mechanism and effects of communicative action.

As we have noted, effective communication is based on an understanding of people, including yourself, and on perceptions relating to motives, emotions, and thoughts. An operational understanding is not difficult to achieve with close friends. But it is quite difficult to understand what a stranger means by his actions, especially when his culture and background differ from your own. Most of us fail to catch important action cues which others transmit constantly. Therefore, as we learn about our own action communication, we will find out more about the communication of others.

The study of communication through actions other than those involving language is fairly recent. Of course, this is not to say that men of all eras have not realized that meaning can be conveyed in different ways. Actors, dancers, writers, and experts on etiquette have all recognized the expressive importance of body movement and the arrangement of objects. But a sort of highbrow prejudice has existed against the study of common—and in that sense, base—forms of communication. This position is represented today by the brilliant amateur psychologist C. Northcote Parkinson, who holds that "grimaces and hand wavings are the resort of the mentally lazy."[4] Proper communication, he implies, involves words; any message which is not couched in words is therefore a slipshod substitute. However, the fact remains that communication often does take place through action language. Behavioral scientists have finally recognized this and have begun in the last 50 years a systematic attempt to analyze **all** levels of communication. Much of what we have included in this book is an exposition of their work.

To approach our topic from a slightly different point of view, every discipline has a terminology of a number of alternative ways of classifying its subject matter. Biologists must learn the meaning of words such as cytoplast and photosynthesis, as well as categories such as phyla and species. The study of action communication has generated its own terminology and a set of categories as well. You will be introduced to these in the next chapter. With this background, we can proceed to look, in Chapters 3 and 4, at the way in which meaning is communicated through action. In Chapter 5 we will discuss the social function of action communication. In Chapters 6 and 7 we will review the manifold ways in which societies differ from one another in the expression of meaning. The last chapter is meant to be a bridge between what you have read and your own experience in communication.

[4] C. Northcote Parkinson, "Parkinson's Law of Human Gesture," **Long Island Press** (May 27, 1970), pp. 25–26.

After you read the following pages, you should be able, in the light of your own experience, to:

1. Look at a communication situation and identify the many different ways in which the participants convey meaning to one another.
2. Recognize the relationships between the various messages which individuals simultaneously transmit.
3. Attribute meaning to an increasingly greater number of human actions.
4. Differentiate between cultural and noncultural influences in the formation of nonverbal codes.
5. Control more effectively the messages which you send to other people.
6. Recognize why the communicative behavior of others is different from your own.

TWO

Definitions, classifications, and problems

The term "communication" has appeared with increasing frequency in periodicals and scholarly journals, and in conversation. As a result, it is rapidly becoming detached from the set of concepts for which it stands because it is so often used in many different ways. An advertising agent is now a "communications specialist." Good or poor communication has become the panacea or scapegoat for both sides of the generation gap. Parents attribute their children's mischief and their adolescents' crimes to the impact of mass communication. Children damn their parents for an inability to communicate with them honestly and meaningfully. Debate on educational policy centers on how teachers and students should communicate with one another. Stretched this way and that by its use in so many different contexts, the word "communication" has lost definitional clarity, yet it is still a useful concept. An individual who does not have a clear idea of what communication includes would have serious difficulty understanding the many ways human interaction takes place. Consequently, this chapter begins with a definition of communication prior to our analysis of communication without words.

Definition of communication

The easiest way to define communication is first to find two people who are talking. We can then point to these individuals and say, "Communication is taking place." From this recognition, together with memories of similar recognitions, we can abstract the common elements of all conversational situations, which are the practical criteria for recognizing a communication situation.

In all conversation—except with ourselves, a special case to be discussed later—at least two people must be involved. One individual must say something and the other must respond in some way so that we will be certain that he has heard what was said. Harold Lasswell constructed a simple scheme for analyzing communication from the minimal requirements for the existence of a communication situation: "Who? Says What? In Which Channel? To Whom? With What Effect?"[1] By changing some of Lasswell's terms, we can construct a preliminary diagrammatic representation of communication (see Figure 2–1). The substitution of the words "sender," "message," "receiver," and "effect" for Lasswell's terms enables us to generalize the diagram to situations other than a conversation between two individuals. We want to allow for possibilities such as a man communicating with a computer or animals communicating between themselves. The term "message" appears twice to represent the physical distortion occurring between sender and receiver. Because of interference (noise, great distance, etc.), what the sender says ($message_1$) may not be what the receiver hears ($message_2$).

We must be careful to recognize that not even the simplest conversation is adequately represented by Figure 2–1. To be more complete, new elements must be designated in the diagram, for **a sender does not transmit one message at a time, but several messages simultaneously.** A sender may vocalize a word, raise his hand, and wink, all at the same time. Each of these actions is a separate message with a particular meaning. And of course the meanings of all these messages are modified by one another. For example, the vocalized phrase "Hello" can be modified by either a frown or a smile. Thus, the several

[1] Harold Lasswell, "The Structure and Function of Communication in Society," in L. Bryson, ed., **The Communication of Ideas** (New York: Harper & Row, Publishers, 1948), p. 29.

messages which an individual sends at one time may complement or contradict one another, but they are rarely disconnected.

Figure 2–1

To sum up, in general, **a communication** is a set of messages which an individual sends at any one time. This definition opens several approaches for analyzing what happens when people interact with one another. What an individual communicates can be described by answering questions such as "What did he say with his face?" "What did he say with his body?" "What did he say with his words?" "Did the facial message fit the body message?" And, since a number of channels are open between participants in an interaction, the analyst can examine the different kinds of interferences which distort the messages of a communication. Noise interferes with aural messages, obstructions with visual messages, and competing smells with olfactory messages. If communication breaks down, did interference on one or more of the channels contribute to this breakdown? (See Figure 2–2.)

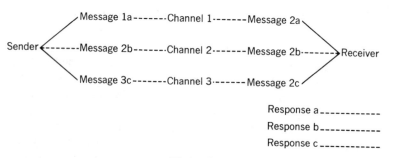

Figure 2–2

If you have followed our description of communication to this point, you may now begin to see some of the ways in which a multi-channeled approach to human interaction may be useful. One of the authors recently found an application of this approach in observing a high school teacher who, following one of the cardinal rules of teaching, was seeking to excite the class about American history by seeming to be excited about the subject herself. Her face beaming with happiness, her voice full of enthusiasm, she rehearsed the events leading to the Boston Massacre. But the students did not respond to these messages probably because predominant in the communication she was sending were messages about boredom. The lethargic way that she moved about the room and her obviously rehearsed gestures indicated an attitude of "Here we go again with this nonsense." The conflict between messages of boredom and messages of enthusiasm made the total communication incoherent. One had the feeling of listening to a four-track stereo with two tracks playing Brahms and two tracks playing The Mothers of Invention. A view of communication as multi-tracked or multi-channeled makes obvious many such instances of conflicting messages which people send out.

To help a person get into synchronization on all levels of communication is extremely difficult. It is usually far less troublesome to remove the interference which distorts messages that are actually sent. Everyone is familiar with the difficulty of speaking in a noisy room, or in a room with bad acoustics. The solution is obvious: throttle some of the folks or move to another room. But what of the less obvious difficulty of talking with someone you cannot see? This often occurs in traditional classrooms where all the students are in rows facing the teacher in the front. If one student in the back wishes to comment on the ideas of someone in the front, many of the students are unable to see him. To the degree that the messages which can only be seen (facial expression and gestures) are important, much of the audience is robbed of the full impact of the communication. In this case, the arrangement of chairs in the room is a very real interference which can be diagnosed only if one is fully aware of the many different messages which compose any communication.

Two other concepts can now be added to the model of communication which we are developing, the first of which centers around the word "stimulus." Figure 2–3 includes a component labeled "initiating stimulus," the perception of which always propels the sender into action. The stimulus might be outside the sender, as in the case of the appearance of another person, or it could arise within the person, as with a pain in the neck or a remembrance of an event during a period of free association. A special label is given to the stimulus which begins communication in order to differentiate it from the stimuli (messages) which are sent and received during interaction, although to the receiver, a message is simply a stimulus. The response of the receiver is a stimulus sent to the sender. Thus, a communication situation exists as long as the participants continue to stimulate one another.

Little more need be said about initiating stimuli, and a great deal has already been said about message stimuli. The third kind of stimulus, the stimulus which the sender gets from the responsive behavior of the receiver, needs elaboration. Individuals engaged in communication watch the reactions of others, converting sensory input into information about the reception of their performance. A speaker at a political rally knows whether he is doing well with the audience by the boos, cheers, cat-calls, and applause which he hears. The same process occurs in any human interaction, with each participant asking himself how his messages are being received by the others. He finds answers by monitoring the responses of others, using the stimuli which they are transmitting to formulate an evaluation of himself. These responses—stimuli to the sender—are called **feedback.** Thus, feedback, the second major element which is represented in Figure 2–3, is the set of stimuli which allows the communicator to determine the effects of his messages. We have already described the feedback which comes to the sender from his receivers—labeled **external feedback.** There exists as well a second type of feedback that begins and ends with the sender of a message—**internal feedback.** Every participant in a communication situation monitors his own output. He makes evaluations of himself because he can hear himself talk and feel himself move. This information is vital. If you never heard yourself in the act of speaking, you would most assuredly fall into some rather strange speech patterns. We are so used to receiving internal feedback that most of it is not even noted consciously. But the effect of self-feedback can be important when mechanical devices are used to amplify the stimuli which we ourselves send. The history teacher mentioned earlier, who sent messages of enthusiasm and boredom at the same time, might well have profited from seeing herself teach on television. Still, nearly everyone can control his output of messages with the sole help of the stimuli which he receives from himself and from his receivers.

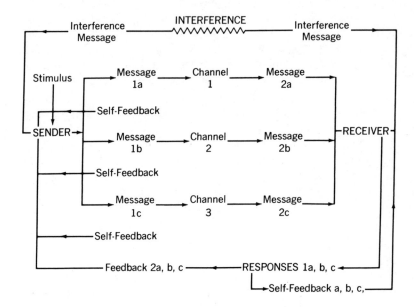

Figure 2–3

We can make the same generalization about the three types of stimuli. The stimuli or raw sense data do not determine an individual's behavior, for every person involved in a communication situation reacts directly to **his** interpretation of the sense data, and only indirectly to the data themselves. This process of interpreting data is known as **perception.** Dean Barnlund puts the concepts of both stimulus and perception into their proper relationship when he argues that the "perception of stimuli, no matter what their origin, is always confined to the nervous system of a single organism."[2] Though communication occurs between people, all stimuli involved in communication are perceived within the person. As biologically similar and socially trained organisms, human beings tend to respond similarly to the same stimuli. But as idiosyncratic beings with different life experiences, individuals can and do interpret the same stimuli quite differently.

[2] Dean Barnlund, **Interpersonal Communication** (Boston: Houghton Mifflin, 1968), p. 8.

Perception is important for each of the types of stimuli involved in communication. What kind of stimulus will cause another to begin to communicate? The answer depends on the way in which individuals have been trained to perceive initiating stimuli. Let us take the case of a person from a small town who rides, for the first time, the New York City subway. Trained to respond to every human being who comes within his proximity, he may very carefully scan each passenger for overtures to communication. When he spies a person smiling at the cartoons in the **Daily News,** he seizes upon the smile as an invitation to begin talking. The **Daily News** reader probably responds with a contemptuous sneer. The newcomer has thus perceived an initiating stimulus which does not, in fact, exist. The city dweller, of course, runs into much the same problem. Since he is trained not to notice or to ignore the behavior of strangers in impersonal surroundings, he fails to perceive initiating stimuli when they are deliberately sent. Our perception of the world, not the sensations received from it, tells us when to begin to communicate.

Messages are processed through the receiver's perceptual equipment: each person adds to and subtracts from the messages which are sent to him. This process in relation to verbal messages is widely understood. When a political candidate says, "I support the democratic way of life," a dozen auditors may interpret the phrases "I support" and "democratic way of life" in a dozen different ways. An important field of investigation called **semantics** is devoted, in part, to the study of why different people perceive different meanings from the same verbal stimuli. A parallel study of the meaning of action language is not nearly so well developed, which is unfortunate because messages without words can also cause difficulty in human interaction. Suppose that you accuse someone of lying. The person replies, "I am not lying." On the verbal level he could mean that he is really telling the truth or that he is not telling a very important lie. Or he could be lying about lying. To check this last hypothesis, you can look at his facial expression and see that he is avoiding eye contact. This avoidance is a message just like spoken words. However, how you perceive this eye message probably depends upon your sensitivity and past experience. The message conveyed by lack of eye contact is just as ambiguous and open to various perceptual treatment as the verbal message.

Feedback, the set of the receiver's responses to a message, cannot be understood apart from the perceptual process. A person's belief about whether he is succeeding in a communication situation is limited only by the reactions of others. Within these limits, an individual can infer many different meanings from reactions to his messages. A speaker cannot hear applause when there is none, but the sound of applause, when it is heard, can be variously interpreted by the speaker as hearty approval of all he has said, ritual affirmation that the speech has come to an end, or shades of meaning in between. We are all forced to construe the reactions of others. Is your friend smiling encouragement, indicating that all is well, and that you should continue to talk? Or is he smiling polite boredom, indicating that you should stop talking or move on to another subject? The way in which you answer these questions is partially dependent upon your own needs and expectations in a particular situation. Feedback, then, consists essentially of material which has meaning only when it is given a personal interpretation by the sender.

No one, of course, spends much time thinking about each of the thousands of stimuli with which he is daily bombarded. Much of the perceptual process occurs outside conscious awareness; consequently, we not only screen out much of the world, but are often blind to our own blindness. As a result, sources of insensitivity and misunderstanding in the communication situation are hidden in the unconscious ways we interpret messages and feedback.

From what we have observed so far, we can derive the following definition: **Human communication is a process in which a sender, triggered by the perception of a stimulus and controlled by feedback, transmits, through channels, a set of messages which are perceived and responded to by a receiver.** Although the diagrams, and the definition drawn from them, systematically describe what happens during interaction, the picture we have drawn is still too simplistic. A prominent student of human communication, Ray Birdwhistell, notes:

> A human being is not a black box with one orifice for emitting a chunk of stuff called **communication** and another for receiving it. And, at the same time, communication is not simply the sum of the bits of information which pass between two people in a given period of time.[3]

The language which we have used to describe communication is linear. That is, it is easy to make statements such as **B** follows **A** and **C**

[3] Ray Birdwhistell, **Kinesics and Context** (Philadelphia: University of Pennsylvania Press, 1970), p. 3.

follows **B,** but it is much more difficult to describe many different events which occur simultaneously, some of which are related to one another and some of which are not. Yet that is precisely what one must do to define communication adequately. The model we have presented is linear: stimulus leads to messages which lead to transmission, and so on, in a continuous circle. However, this model represents the complexity of communication about as well as a stick drawing represents a man. In actual communication, all parties involved are, at the same time, senders and receivers—that is, everyone is simultaneously emitting and interpreting behaviors, his own as well as those of others. Tremendous amounts of information are being relayed through the system. Birdwhistell estimates that in order to record the signals sent out by two human infants, a data bank would have to take note of 10,000 bits of information per second.[4] Therefore, because of the limits of language in relation to the complexity of the phenomenon of communication, no definition can more than hint at what occurs during human transactions.

As we have said, we can be certain that communication does involve more than the simple interchange of words. This, in fact, is the central justification for using as amorphous a term as communication. Language, the system of meaning on which vocal productions are based, is naturally at center stage when individuals study speech. All other human behaviors are important only to the extent that they modify the meanings transmitted through speech. But to study communication is to examine all the ways in which human beings send information and interpret and integrate their actions and feelings. Once the concept of communication is adopted, speech is immediately placed in perspective, for although it is the most complex message form, speech is not necessarily the most common. In fact, verbal messages may carry far less impact than other message forms. One researcher, Albert Mehrabian, estimates that in the situations which he examined, only 7 percent of the total impact of a communication was verbal. Another 38 percent of impact he attributed to the ways in which the words were said, and the remainder, 55 percent of impact, came from facial expressions.[5] These numerical proportions unfortunately belie the obvious. The factors which contribute to the total impact of any given message depend upon the purpose and context

[4] **Ibid.**
[5] Albert Mehrabian, "Communication Without Words," **Psychology Today,** II (September 1968), 53.

of the interaction, and upon the perceptions of the interactants. When a person says "Hello" the impact of the verbal message may be far less than the cheery tone with which the word is said and the happy smile on the face of the sender. But when an instructor is giving directions on how to take a test, the verbal messages may be far more important than any other part of the communication. If we take into account these variables, Mehrabian's basic contention can still be tentatively accepted: There is far more to communication than the sending and receiving of verbal messages.

Definition of nonverbal communication

All communication except that which is coded in words is generally referred to as **nonverbal communication**. This rubric is in one way unsatisfactory. The term "nonverbal" aggregates different kinds of behavior which have in common only the quality of not being structured by a linguistic system. Like the term "nonhuman," which covers an infinity of life forms from protozoa to gorillas, "nonverbal" denotes that which is **not** included in the concept "verbal", but it tells little about what **is** included. Still, this commonly accepted designation for the field which we wish to discuss provides a starting point. The inclusion of the term "communication" suggests that what has been previously said about communication applies fully to messages without words. The model and the definition apply to all transfers of meaning between individuals. The next step is obvious—verbal and nonverbal communicative behavior must be distinguished from one another.

Up to this point, we have used several substitute terms for nonverbal communication: action communication, action language, and the like. In a rigorous sense, it is not accurate to think of nonverbal communication as involving body acts—"body language" is the phrase in vogue—and verbal behavior as not involving action. Even verbal communication involves action. "You fill your lungs with wind and shake a little slit in your throat, and make mouths, and that shakes the air."[6] The real distinction between verbal and nonverbal communicative behavior lies in the system by which action is organized. Verbal behavior is organized by language systems, whereas nonverbal behavior is not.

[6] George DuMaurier, **Peter Ibbetson** (New York: Harper & Brothers, 1931), p. 387.

Language is arbitrary, tightly organized, and self-reflexive. The symbols of language—speech sounds or the scratches called writing —are arbitrarily given meaning in a language system. There is no inherent reason why the sound "boy" should refer to a male child. In fact, the same meaning can be transmitted by sounds like "garcon" or "knaben." However, although the meaning of some nonverbal signs is arbitrarily chosen, many gestures are somehow directly linked to the idea which they represent. But even in this realm there are a wide variety of responses. For example, how one points is arbitrary. Members of some cultures point with their entire head, or with their lips, or, as in our culture, with the arms and fingers. But pointing always involves the movement of part of the body in the direction being designated. Thus, the act of pointing is not arbitrary. The number of nonverbal clues which have inherent meaning could be multiplied many times, but the basic point is that much nonverbal behavior is not arbitrarily meaningful and, in this way, is different from verbal behavior.

The symbols of language are structured into tight patterns, one of which English grammar describes. Interestingly, investigators have recently found unnoticed patterns in nonverbal behavior as well, suggesting that a "grammar" of body movement may exist. Although this kind of study can be extremely useful, as we shall see shortly, no clear demonstration has yet been made that nonverbal behaviors can be related to one another in the same way that words in a language can be related through the grammar of that language.

Verbal expressions are self-reflexive; in other words, language can be used to talk about language. If a person were to say, " 'I ain't got no car' ain't good grammar," he would be using (bad) language to talk about (bad) language. But a wave of the hand cannot be used to analyze a wave of the hand. Since "language is language only if it can be used for language analysis,"[7] nonverbal acts, lacking self-reflexiveness, are different from verbal acts.

The comparison of ways in which verbal messages differ from nonverbal messages has been extended by Jurgen Ruesch, a pioneer investigator in nonverbal communication. The distinctions which he draws are important for understanding the different levels of human interaction. He notes that nonverbal expressions are continuous func-

[7] Joseph DeVito, **Psychology of Speech and Language** (New York: Random House, Inc., 1970), p. 8.

tions; for example, a person's hand is almost constantly in motion. Whereas sounds and letters have discrete beginnings and ends, and a person can therefore choose not to talk, he cannot, while he is with others, choose not to communicate nonverbally. Ruesch continues by explaining that nonverbal cues can be received through many different sense organs simultaneously, for a person can, in one moment, feel, smell, see, and hear one message source. Verbal communication, however, can be received by far fewer types of sense receptors. One only sees written verbal messages and one only hears oral verbal messages. Consequently, one is more likely to receive many different nonverbal cues simultaneously than to receive and comprehend two verbal messages at the same time.[8]

A last, but pragmatically important distinction, is based on the content of what is communicated verbally and nonverbally. In general, verbal communication has a proportionately larger cognitive content than nonverbal communication, for language can easily designate objects and relationships whereas nonverbal communication, in many instances, is better suited for the projection of emotional states. Although verbal messages with strong emotional appeals can be formulated, the unskilled person often has difficulty using language in this way. Rather, most people act out their strong feelings nonverbally. Indeed, just as the unskilled communicator has difficulty putting his feelings into words, none but the very skilled can avoid putting emotions into their actions.

Types of nonverbal communication

Many different ways have been proposed for classifying the major kinds of human expressions which do not involve the use of words because investigators study this wide range of expressive behavior with different purposes in mind. Before we comment directly on the specific categories which have been proposed by various researchers, let us take a brief look at a broad-gauge classificatory scheme to help give you a general idea of what is included in the concept of nonverbal communication.

The simplest scheme of classification has been proposed by Jurgen Ruesch and Weldon Kees. They allow for three distinct categories of

[8] Jurgen Ruesch, "Nonverbal Language," in Robert Cathcart and Larry Samovar, eds., **Small Group Communication** (Dubuque: Brown, 1970), pp. 260–63.

nonverbal expression. The first, **sign language,** is the substitution of gestures for words, numbers, and punctuation signs. The most complete sign language is the gestural system used by the deaf. However, many other gestures are simple equivalents for verbal phrases; for example, the forefinger and thumb forming a circle with the other fingers extended is a substitute for the phrase "OK." Second, **action language** embraces all those movements which are not used solely as signals. Walking is an example of action language which serves the dual function of locomotion and of telling others about the walker. Eating, drinking, moving the hands, driving a car, and making love are activities with both instrumental and communicative significance. And third, **object language** is the display of material things, either intentionally or unintentionally, which has the effect of expressing something about the displayer. Clothes, furniture, architectural arrangements, the human body itself can all be objects for expressive display.[9]

The Ruesch and Kees scheme clarifies what is to be included in the study of nonverbal communication. All human movement is included in one of their three categories. However, by including all species of communicative behavior in only these three categories, they have put together widely dissimilar phenomena. A more discriminating system is obviously needed. Unfortunately, few students of communication seem interested in developing more elaborate taxonomies of expression. Researchers tend to analyze that behavior which interests them, allowing only minimal time for definitional exercises. In order to go beyond extremely general classifications, then, we should review the types of relevant behavior which investigators have defined and analyzed.

Paralanguage. Extensive research has been done on the two **nonverbal components of the speech act:** voice set and nonverbal vocalizations. Taken together, these components are called **paralanguage.** Voice set is important for both verbal and nonverbal vocalizations; some of the qualities by which it can be measured are intensity (volume), pitch, resonance, rate, and rhythm. Voice set is determined by the speaker's physical and psychological condition, and differences in voice set become the basis for social categorization. Certain

[9] Jurgen Ruesch and Weldon Kees, **Nonverbal Communication: Notes on the Visual Perception of Human Relations** (Berkeley: University of California Press, 1956), p. 189.

kinds of voice sets are strongly identified with age and sex groups, with body conditions, with physique, and with status in a group. For example, in our society, there is a clear notion of the difference between a masculine and feminine voice; an ill person is presumed to sound one way, a healthy person another; and a person's desire to be dominant or submissive in a group can often be deduced by the sound of his voice. Personality characteristics are often ascribed on the basis of vocal qualifiers. A brash bore is a loud mouth, a timid soul speaks softly; an excitable person at times of stress utters words at a greater rate and at a higher pitch than normally.

Nonverbal vocalizations are divided into three types: (1) vocal characterizers; (2) vocal qualifiers; (3) vocal segregates. Laughing and sobbing while speaking are **vocal characterizers.** So are audibly yawning, or moaning, or belching. **Vocal qualifiers** consist of momentary variations of pitch or volume. **Vocal segregates** are sounds or silences which appear between the articulation of words, such as "uh's," "ah's," "mmmm's," and the like. Also included are the periods of nonvocalization during an utterance, which can have powerful communicative meaning. A person who is trying to foster an appearance of calm deliberation will often make a point of pausing between words.

Paralinguistic expressions are usually related to an individual's choice of linguistic expression—his use of words and his grammar. Thus, a communicator can choose to use long or short sentences, to use a large or small vocabulary, or to employ the present or past tense. And, as you have just seen, a choice can be made between high or low pitch, or between the use of few or many vocal segregates. Both the verbal and nonverbal choices which an individual makes create a composite message about him:

> A self-confident person may speak in relatively simple sentences with well controlled pitch and volume, and with few sighs or nervous coughs. An insecure person, on the other hand, may speak in complex, involved or even unfinished sentences, with poor pitch and volume control, and with frequent nervous mannerisms.[10]

These differences in the related verbal and nonverbal components of an oral communication are important because they can have a strong

---

[10] George Mahl and Gene Schulze, "Psychological Research in the Extralinguistic Area," in Thomas Sebeok **et al.,** eds., **Approaches to Semiotics** (The Hague: Mouton, 1964), p. 51.

impact on the listener. For example, high pitch and long pauses (paralinguistic form) together with long sentences (linguistic form) often bore and annoy listeners.

Body movements are a second group of nonverbal expressions. To be precise, the sending of vocal nonverbal messages is also body movement. A great many discrete actions are involved in saying "ugh" or in coughing. The distinction we want to draw here is that whereas paralinguistic expressions are vocalized, the second group of movements are not. That is, paralinguistic expressions are **heard,** but other body actions with expressive content are **seen.** Facial expressions and hand gestures are the most familiar kinds of body movement in this second group.

One way of describing body communication is to locate the area of the body which sends the message. Thus, one might say that body action is divisible into facial expressions, whole head movements, gestures (movements of the extremities), trunk movements, and posture (whole body movement). However, this sort of classification does not reveal much about the nature or function of body communication.

A fairly elaborate scheme for classifying body action has been proposed by Paul Ekman and Wallace Friesen.[11] They argue that there are basically five types of body expressions: (1) emblems, (2) illustrators, (3) regulators, (4) affect displays, and (5) adaptors. Their category of **emblems** is very similar to Ruesch and Kees's classification, "sign language." For Ekman and Friesen, emblems are usually gestural equivalents of a word or phrase. For example, the phrase "come here" can easily be replaced by a familiar motion which means the same thing. Emblematic movements most frequently occur when the verbal channel is blocked. A ground controller can gesture a pilot into the proper position when the aircraft approaches so close that its sound makes oral communication impossible. The number of "obscene emblems" such as the middle finger pointing up suggests that there may be greater inhibition against vocalizing certain phrases than against using gestural equivalents. The meaning of many emblems is purely arbitrary; as an example, twirling the forefinger around the temple to indicate that another person is "nuts" has no visual connection with either the concept of madness or with the acts of the

---

[11] Paul Ekman and Wallace Friesen, "The Repertoire of Nonverbal Behavior: Categories, Origins, Usage, and Coding," **Semiotics,** I (1969), 63–92.

insane. In fact, Anglo-Americans of another era arbitrarily chose to convey the same idea by placing the forefinger next to the nose. However, as we noted above, not all emblematic gestures are visually detached from their referents. In fact, the emblematic representations for many body acts have some visual relation to the acts. Moreover, emblematic gestures are learned in the same way that languages are learned—by imitation.

Illustrators are directly linked to speech, for they "illustrate" what is being said orally. People speak rhythmically and, in addition, they may gesture in time to their vocalization. A gesture can add emphasis to a particular part of a phrase. Illustrators also express logical relations or directions, and spatial relationships. For example, few speakers can keep their hands still when uttering phrases such as, "Let us all unite in a common crusade," "I shall move forward to the next point," or "They came from afar." Movements in which an individual points at an object to which he is verbally referring, or in which he depicts a bodily movement about which he is talking, are also illustrators. Some illustrators—acts which designate or depict—can usually stand alone, without verbal support. However, other illustrators—those emphasizing rhythm or relationship—can only be understood in connection with the verbal message. One learns to use illustrators through imitation, and because they are socially learned, they are also socially variable. Class or ethnic group membership is easily betrayed by the kinds of illustrators an individual uses. Some speech teachers often try to short-circuit this process of imitative learning by requiring their students to use only relatively few illustrators, and those are rigidly prescribed.

Regulators are actions which serve to control oral interaction. "They tell the speaker to continue, repeat, elaborate, hurry up, become more interesting, less salacious. . . . They can tell the listener to pay special attention, to wait just a minute more, to talk, etc."[12] Most regulators, like most illustrators, cannot be understood apart from the verbal messages being exchanged. Leaning forward or backward, breaking eye contact, head nodding, and raising the eyebrows are all classified as regulators. How we use regulators depends on the knowledge we gain through observation.

Affect displays are body expressions which indicate the emotional

[12] **Ibid.,** p. 82.

state of the communicator. Since facial expressions are the principal way most humans convey their feelings, a face that shows anger, fear, or disgust is displaying an affective state. Unlike body movements in the previous three categories, affect displays are not tightly bound to verbal expressions. Further, affect displays tend to be less consciously controllable than the previous three types. Consequently, many people carefully watch affect displays as a way of checking up on the veracity of verbal statements.

Adaptors are movements we first learned in childhood which were part of a patterned activity with an instrumental purpose. You may have noticed an individual during a conversation wipe his mouth on the back of his hand. This action was once part of a grooming pattern which he was trained to follow. As an adult, however, he is using this isolated movement to relieve stress, or to put on a better face. There are three types of adaptors: (1) **self-adaptors,** such as mouth wiping, remnants of a learned activity toward one's own body; (2) **alter-adaptors,** such as movements learned in the process of manipulating material things; and (3) **object-adaptors,** such as using a tool, or smoking, gestures which indicate re-arrangement. Each of these kinds of adaptor movements is theoretically performed without one's awareness. They are not generally noticed or, at least, commented upon, by others. To the trained eye, however, adaptors indicate much about their performer's socialization experience and emotional state.

Kinesics. In constructing the system just described, Ekman and Friesen attempt to account for the origin, use, and meaning of expressive body movement. A second system for classifying body action, formulated by Ray Birdwhistell, is quite different in its purpose. Birdwhistell coined the term **kinesics,** which is today largely synonymous with the study of all body movement, for the "study of the visual aspects of nonverbal, interpersonal communication." The method which Birdwhistell employs to investigate kinesic phenomena closely follows that used by students of language. Just as linguists try to discover the structure of a new language, kinesiologists attempt to find a set of recurrent relationships between various body movements. Just as phoneticians study the sounds which the human vocal apparatus is capable of uttering, kinesiologists first determine what movements the body is capable of making. This field of study is called **prekinesics.** But just as all sounds are not meaningful, not all movements are expressive. We call the study of those movements which are expressive **microkinesics.** Further, the way in which movements form a part of the interactional life of a culture is the province of **social kinesics**—the study of the meaning of specific movements in a particular culture.

The three levels of kinesic investigation can best be explained with reference to an early experiment conducted by Birdwhistell, who began with the premise that the human eyelid is capable of innumerable positions. However, persons viewing a human face can only discriminate among 11 different positions, and further, in our culture, only four eyelid positions seem to alter perception of one's facial expression. The positions of which the eyelid is capable is the object of prekinesic investigation, discriminable and meaningful positions are investigated by microkinesiologists, and the student of social kinesics investigates the way eyelid position is important in social interaction.[13]

Proxemics. So far we have discussed two broad kinds of nonverbal communication: paralinguistics and kinesics. A third kind of nonverbal communication involves the relationships between the communicator's body and other people or objects in the environment; the study of these is called **proxemics,** and the key concept is space. One of the most important investigators in this field, Edward Hall, notes that man's use of space is communicative.[14] For example, how far interactants stand from one another indicates their degree of familiarity and the purpose of their communication. Put another way, individuals send messages by placing themselves in certain spatial relations with one another. Characterizations such as, "Jones is too intimate," or, "Smith is standoffish," are probably statements about spatial relationships. Proxemic relationships reflect the total culture of a society. When you next walk into a classroom or an office, look around to see what the room tells you about the people who occupy it. Do some people have different kinds of spaces allotted to them? Who in the room is allowed to communicate with whom, and at what distance? What do the answers to these questions tell you about current views toward the nature of education or business, about the

[13] Ray Birdwhistell, "Background to Kinesics," **ETC,** XIII (1955), 10–18; **idem,** "Kinesics and Communication," in Edmund Carpenter and Marshall McLuhan, eds., **Explorations in Communication** (Boston: Beacon Press, 1960), pp. 54–64.
[14] Edward Hall, **Hidden Dimension** (Garden City, N.Y.: Doubleday & Company, Inc., 1966), pp. 1–6.

roles to which individuals are assigned, and about the hierarchy of status in the organization? The manipulation of objects in relation to spacing needs must be clearly distinguished from object manipulation by which human beings attempt to extend their self-expression by setting their environment in a certain order. Some examples of this latter behavior have already been given: wearing certain clothes, cleaning a house, or arranging items on a shelf. This manipulation of the physical world for expressive purposes has not been given a neat rubric, so borrowing from theatrical jargon, we shall call this form of nonverbal communication **property management.**

From the last few pages, you should have sensed that the study of nonverbal communication has not yet been neatly defined and structured. Moreover, the welter of so many terms is an indication of the innumerable, overlapping ways open through which one human being contacts another.

Issues in defining nonverbal communication

Nonverbal communication does not include language use, but it does include the various vocal, somatic, and manipulative behaviors just discussed. There is little problem in distinguishing stimuli which are verbal messages from those which are not. However, distinguishing stimuli which carry nonverbal meaning from stimuli which are not part of the communicative process is more difficult. How can nonverbal **messages** be distinguished from the rest of the nonverbal world? We must consider the following three issues: environment, expert perception, and intent.

The physical world is full of meaning. Each species perceives acutely a limited set of these meanings. The caterpillar senses fine gradations in the texture of leaves which allow him to distinguish food from poison. Fish depend upon minute changes in water temperature to steer them on their migrations. Man responds to the smell of sizzling steak. Do these acts of perception indicate that animals communicate with their inorganic environment? The answer is "no" if communication is defined as a process of responses. Evaluation of the world should not be confused with communication. Communication between man and steak proceeds in one direction, from stimulus-object to respondent-organism. Nothing in man's behavior will cause the steak to behave differently.

We must attach a reservation to this distinction between the physical world, which might meaningfully be perceived, and nonverbal cues. When they construct messages, individuals manipulate objects. For example, before friends visit, you clean your house to create (probably) an artificial impression of neatness, in the hope that guests will respond favorably. Your home is a carefully prepared message, and your guests' behavior, labeled feedback in our earlier model, indicates an evaluation of the message. But note carefully: communication does not occur between clean floor and guests. It occurs between you and your guests through the medium of object display.

Individuals differ in their perception of nonverbal signs. A feature of the environment will act as a message only if it is recognized as such by its recipient. For example, whereas a psychiatrist can find actions which are symptomatic of a patient's disorder, the patient's friends ignore these same actions completely. A baseball manager can often tell whether his pitcher is tired from the way he steps off the rubber, although the fans in the bleachers are totally oblivious to this cue. Both the psychiatrist and the baseball manager, because of their expertise, will recognize and respond to messages that others do not notice. Thus, a nonverbal message to one person may not be a message to another. For the most part, we will discuss behaviors which are meaningful to nonexperts participating in the communication situation, although this general orientation must again be qualified. First, individuals within any culture possess varying degrees of ability to perceive nonverbal messages. These individual differences are a significant variable to be examined later. Second, by systematically studying nonverbal communication, you may begin to recognize a much wider range of messages than before. Learning to be a perceptive communicator means, in part, increasing your sensitivity to the messages which others send.

We have now argued that communication must be interactive, that is, both the **sender** and the **receiver** of messages must be able to respond to one another. Further, a nonverbal message must be perceived as such by the recipient of the communication. Last, we wish to propose that a person may communicate nonverbally whether he intends to or not. There is, understandably, debate over this contention. Franklin Fearing speaks for a number of social scientists when he argues that only those actions which are intended to communicate can be subsumed under the concept of communication. The basis of his argument lies in a distinction between coping behavior and expressive behavior. **Coping behavior** is characteristically easily controlled, designed to cause changes in the environment, and highly conscious. Talking and making the motion which denotes "come here" are examples of coping behaviors which are communicative. **Expressive behavior** is an involuntary action by an organism which indicates to others something about that organism. One example is blushing from embarrassment. By communication, Fearing means coping behavior, but not uncontrollable, nonconscious behavior.[15]

The distinction between coping and expressive behavior is not, in our opinion, a useful one for defining nonverbal communication. Ruesch and Kees argue that

> distinctions cannot be made between the adaptive actions that implement homeostatic needs [expressive or autistic acts] and communicative actions that increase a person's knowledge or convey information to others or achieve a calculated effect. Although assumptions are continually being made that clear-cut lines of demarcation exist between unintentional expression on one hand and intentional communication on the other, such lines of demarcation are impossible to maintain scientifically.

In short, there is no way operationally to designate one set of actions in an interaction as consciously motivated. Further, the most important information which passes between interactants is often of the type that Fearing calls expressive. Ruesch and Kees continue by noting that

> Not infrequently it can be observed that silent actions implemented through contractions of the smooth or striped muscles can be highly informative whereas statements made through words remain inconsequential or are hardly noticed."[16]

The behaviors which should be included in a discussion of nonverbal communication are those which act as messages on a receiver. Using this criterion, the function, rather than the motivation for an act, is emphasized. This standard is the only one which provides an objective measurement. One can never be certain of the sender's

---

[15] Franklin Fearing, "Toward a Psychological Theory of Human Communication," **Journal of Personality,** XXII (1953), 74.
[16] Ruesch and Kees, **Nonverbal Communication,** p. 48.

state of awareness, but whether a receiver responds or not can, conceivably, be measured.

If we consider communication to be the totality of ways in which men interact with one another, we can proceed to gain a more specific understanding of the dynamics which give rise to communication. In the next two chapters, the psychological and physiological nature of man as both sender and receiver of communication will be examined.

THREE

Nonverbal meaning: a behavioral approach

The publisher's advertisement for a recent best seller on nonverbal communication claims that the author "teaches you how to penetrate the personal secrets both of strangers and intimates, by correctly reading their Body Language." A reviewer, angry with the book, described it as a study in obfuscation. She suggested that although the author purported that nonverbal cues mean something, he was unable to say just which cues mean what.[1] The reviewer was, presumably, disappointed in not finding what had been promised, a dictionary of expressive movement. Now, to construct a dictionary inclusive of very few movements is possible; one sprightly offering of this kind is the **Supplemento al Dizionario Italiano,** a word and picture explanation of a few dozen common Italian gestures. The book explains, for example, that when "the flat hand, palm downwards, makes a rapid slashing movement across the throat, to suggest a blade," the message conveyed is a "threat."[2] Movements which are the equivalents of verbal phrases can be defined in this way. However, the systematic definition

---

[1] Marcia Seligson, "American Notebook," **The New York Times Book Review** (October 25, 1970), p. 32.
[2] Bruno Munari, **Supplemento al Dizionario Italiano** (Milan: Muggiani Editore, 1963), pp. 66–67.

of what Ekman and Friesen call emblems is relatively useless. Millions of Americans did not run to their **Supplemento** to find out what Mayor Daley meant by his throat-slashing signs at the 1968 Decomratic convention. Their effort would have gotten them the wrong information anyway, since this particular movement means one thing in Milan and something else in Chicago. More important, no dictionary of emblems, except perhaps one covering the occult signs of secret societies, will allow one to penetrate anyone's deepest secrets. Gestural substitutes for words are used with the same high degree of conscious awareness as the words themselves. No one is going to simply let slip an "Up yours."

Symbols and signs

The most revealing nonverbal cues cannot be so easily defined as words or the gestural equivalents of words. Verbal expression is symbolic. **Symbols** convey meaning through arbitrary connections with the thoughts they represent. The word "cuckold" stands for a category of husbands whose wives are unfaithful, and thus, in order to define cuckold, the characteristics of cuckolds must be known. That is precisely what we did in the last sentence, perhaps adding a new and useful word to your vocabulary. One person can call another a cuckold by saying "You, sir, are a cuckold" or by making a specific hand gesture, the index and little finger held straight up, the middle fingers placed in the palm. Either way, he is engaging in symbolic or verbal communication. **Signs** are inherently connected with what they represent. A cough is a sign of a cold, and it is also part of having a cold. Most nonverbal messages can be called signs. An angry look is a sign of anger, and it is also part of being angry. The difficulty of defining signs is that their meaning is more contextual than that of symbols. Most words have only a few meanings, depending upon who is using them in which circumstances. But the wrinkling of a nose is a sign which can have a thousand different meanings, each of which is dependent upon the set of signs which accompany it, the personality of the wrinkler, and the context of the wrinkling. For this reason, it is hard to assign general meaning to any isolated nonverbal sign, even though a specific meaning in a particular context is obvious. We would hazard no guess about what nose wrinkling means in general, but few people in the course of conversation would take umbrage at a sentence such as, "Joan is wrinkling her nose because she can't stand the smell of fried mushrooms."

Although we are unable to make categorical statements such as, "An arched eyebrow means anger," we can say what certain signs **do** in the communication situation. Broadly, nonverbal messages have three overlapping functions: (1) to clarify, confirm, or deny verbal messages; (2) to reveal the attitudes, emotions, and physical state of the sender; and (3) to define the individual's social identity. The remainder of this chapter and the whole of the next will be devoted to how nonverbal signs clarify verbal statements and express the feelings of the communicator.

The relation between verbal and nonverbal messages has already been mentioned. We indicated that vocal variations and gestures influence the interpretation of words used in speech. Vocalization and voice set can be relatively emotion-free, simply helping the receiver understand the verbal message better. A slow rate of speech, pauses, and clear pronunciation are variations which make clear the words being sent. Gestures can also clarify the verbal content of a communication without adding important emotional overtones. Movements which Ekman and Friesen call Illustrators and Regulators are essentially clarificatory.

Judgment of vocal expression

The different ways words are spoken not only clarify but add an emotional connotation to verbal messages. Vocal expressions are an important form of affective display. In one experiment on the vocal expressions of emotion, eight persons were asked to recite the alphabet so as to convey feelings of anger, fear, jealousy, happiness, and love. The alphabet was chosen so that the sounds could be content free and interpretation of what was being said could thus not be contaminated by an overt verbal message. Thirty subjects were asked to listen to these recitations and, using a list of words denoting emotions, to label the feeling being expressed. Emotions were said to be correctly identified when the sender of the vocal messages and its receiver, the subject, were in agreement. The result of the experiment was that agreement was attained with a frequency far above chance. You can confirm this part of the research findings yourself by informally replicating this experiment. Tape-record a list of such

nonsense words as zork, gomph, wibble, comph, rappel, and aribellen-
tonic. Then, during the course of the taping, recite your list in a number of different ways, attempting with each recitation to express a
particular feeling. When you play the completed tape to friends, ask
them to identify the different emotions that you were attempting
to convey. If all goes well, some people will be very good at interpreting the tape, although others will be unsuccessful; for, as the
original experimenters found, individuals vary in their ability to discriminate nonverbal cues. They felt that there are "wide individual
differences in the accuracy with which persons express and judge
feelings."[3] This finding is just as important as the confirmation of the
idea that emotions can be expressed vocally. A communicator is not
operating a mechanical system in which certain behavior will trigger
an invariant response; rather, the communicator, imperfectly able to
control his own behavior, sends messages which are imperfectly perceived by others.

Judgment of facial expression

Researchers have returned again and again to the question of what
emotional messages may be correctly perceived. And the most
developed tradition of investigation is in the judgment of facial expression. Experimental research by psychologists in this field began
in the second decade of the twentieth century when investigators
questioned the generally assumed ability of people to make accurate
judgments about the emotive meaning of facial expressions. Such
clichés as "an angry look" or "a happy smile" presuppose one's
ability to infer the existence of an emotion from an outward behavioral
sign. Agreement was reached among psychologists by the 1940s that
emotion could not be judged from facial expression alone, for the
apparent ability to do so rested on an interpretation of all the information in a situation. Suppose that you drop your great-aunt's Ming
vase. You look at her face and judge that she is angry. That judgment,
so it was maintained, is not an interpretation of her face but an
anticipation of her emotional state based on the situation. You could
not, it was thought, make the same judgment if a psychologist showed
you a series of pictures of Aunt Lizzie and asked you to judge what she

[3] Joel R. Davitz and Lois Jean Davitz, "The Communication of Feelings by Con-
tent-Free Speech," **Journal of Communication**, IX (1959), 6–13.

was expressing in each. However, recent studies provide evidence to challenge this interpretation of the data. At least seven categories of emotion can be accurately detected from facial expressions: happiness, surprise, fear, anger, sadness, disgust/contempt, and interest.[4]

"Judgment studies" are the most popular form of research on facial expression. In these experiments, facial behavior is defined as the stimulus. In order to conclude that the meaning of a facial expression has been accurately perceived, subjects in the experiment must either agree about the emotion which is expressed or be able to distinguish between various facial behaviors emitted under different circumstances. In most experiments, subjects are presented with a series of still photographs, and are asked to apply to each photograph one of a list of terms denoting various emotions. Within this general format, designs differ in a number of ways. In some experiments, the photographs are of actors who have been asked to simulate a series of emotions. In others, individuals are photographed in an act designed to simulate an emotional reaction—disgust, for example, while decapitating a live rat. Instead of using still photographs, some experimenters employ live models or movie sequences. Results are usually expressed in two forms: some investigators try to validate emotion categories, such as those listed at the end of the previous paragraph, and others describe expressions of emotion along several continua, from grief to joy, or from relaxation to alertness.

One of the most influential of the early judgment studies pointed to the conclusion that meaning cannot be attributed to facial expression. The experimenter, Carney Landis, photographed 25 persons in a series of 17 situations which included, among others, listening to music, looking at pornographic pictures, and smelling ammonia. After each experience, the subject was asked to write a brief introspective report on his reaction. Four of the original 25 subjects were later asked to remember each situation and pose with an appropriate facial expression. Forty-two other subjects were then asked to judge the photographs, stating in their own words the emotion they thought was felt by the stimulus person, the situation which probably elicited the emotion, and their feeling of certainty about the judgment which they

[4] This list is taken from Paul Ekman, Wallace Friesen, and Phoebe Ellsworth, **Emotion in the Human Face: Guidelines for Research and a Review of Findings** (Elmsford, N.Y.: Pergamon Press, forthcoming), used with the permission of the authors. The authors are also indebted to this book for a number of insights into the structure and findings in this field.

had made. Landis concluded that facial expression has little emotive meaning because most judgments were irrelevant to the actual and posed situations, and to the introspective reports made during the initial phase of the experiment.[5]

The Landis experiments can be criticized on several grounds. First, Landis structured his laboratory work in such a way that there was only a brief time lapse between situations. Consequently, there was a carry-over of emotion from one situation to the next, making it impossible to distinguish reactions which were, in fact, overlapping. Second, the situations may not have evoked the same emotions in each person, or may have elicited several emotions simultaneously. In either case, agreement on a single judgment among the subjects would be extremely unlikely. Third, Landis may have encouraged the masking of facial reactions. Each person knew that he was being photographed, and was aware of the purpose of the experiment. J. C. Coleman, in an experiment with a somewhat different purpose and design, corrected the faults in Landis's procedures and arrived at results which support the hypothesis that facial expression of emotion can be accurately judged.[6]

Recent research on the nonverbal expression of emotion, then, is tending once again toward the ancient notion and the general belief that the human body transmits signs which can be interpreted with some confidence by an observer. But precisely which cues are meaningful remains a subject of debate. Psychologists have investigated this question using much the same method they employ in judgment studies. Although they continue to use either still photographs or motion pictures, they have modified the stimulus by blocking out parts of the face. In the typical experiment, subjects might be divided into three groups, the first group to judge the whole face, the second the bottom half of the face, and the third the top half of the face. If, for any given emotion, the first group agrees with one of the other groups, and the remaining group seems to have no clue to the emotion expressed, then one area of the face may be said to be more expressive of that particular emotion than the other. Although such research could conceivably indicate the general location or configuration of

[5] Carney Landis, "The Interpretation of Facial Expression in Emotion," **Journal of General Psychology,** II (1929), 59–72.
[6] J. C. Coleman, "Facial Expressions of Emotion," **Psychological Monographs,** LXIII (1949), 1–32.

expressive actions, results have been so contradictory that no definite conclusions can be drawn.[7]

Another approach to the judgment of facial expression comes from the study of kinesics. We mentioned in the previous chapter that one of the subdivisions of kinesics is called microkinesics. Individuals interested in microkinesics have sought to discover ranges of action which can be said to carry perceptual cues. For example, when an eyelid minutely changes position, an observer will probably not notice that a change has taken place, but after a greater shift, the observer can say that one position is different from another. These differences which can be perceived Birdwhistell calls **kines,** which can be represented by written symbols in a notational system which approximates that used for describing vocal phenomena. Paralinguists, for example, note a southern drawl as ⌢ . Similarly, Birdwhistell constructed a notational system in which an open eye could be indicated by the sign ⊂⊃ , the closed eye by the sign ⸻ .᾿Obviously, no single kine has a meaning in itself. Rather, actions which have meaning are composed of a number of kines which occur in some fixed relation to one another. These constellations of related actions Birdwhistell calls **kinemorphs.** What messages, then, do these kinemorphs carry? In one experiment subjects were shown notations representing the major facial features: two representing the eyelids, two the eyebrows, one the nose, and one the mouth. In a single run of the experiment, changing the noted position of the eyelids did not affect overall judgment of expression, but changing the noted position of the mouth did. A conclusion which could be drawn from this sort of experiment is that for certain expressions or kinemorphs eyelid position is less important than mouth position.[8] However, such statements must be qualified by the reservation that judgment of highly abstracted symbols might have little relation to judgment of the actual expressions they represent. Further, this format for the study of kinesics has not produced a clear description of kinemorphs, nor has it begun to supply any definitive meanings for body motion.

Voices and faces, then, can be accurately judged, for certain emotions are revealed by either vocal or visual cues. But are the same

[7] Ekman, Friesen, and Ellsworth, **Emotion in the Human Face.**
[8] Ray Birdwhistell, "Kinesics and Communication," in Edmund Carpenter and Marshall McLuhan, eds., **Explorations in Communication** (Boston: Beacon Press, 1960), pp. 56–57.

emotions communicated by both face and voice? Hypothetically, the face could be very expressive of fear, the voice of anger. The face, however, could indicate nothing about anger, and the voice nothing about fear. An experiment by Williams and Sundene tends to refute this hypothesis. They found that face and voice transmit some of the same information: subjects could tell from either visual or vocal cues whether an individual is feeling pleasure or pain, whether he is pleasant or unpleasant, lenient or severe.[9] This does not mean, however, that emotions are communicated just as effectively in both modes. Levitt, for example, has found that joy is most accurately judged from faces, and fear from the voice.[10]

Twenty-two years ago, the anthropologist Edward Sapir generalized about knowledge of nonverbal communication. He wrote that "we respond to gestures with an extreme alertness and, one might say, in accordance with an elaborate and secret code that is written nowhere, known by none, and understood by all."[11] After years of research, we have found that there is indeed an elaborate code for meaningful expression which is widely understood. But the code, for the most part, remains unbroken. This is not grounds, however, for abandoning the study of the emotional meaning of nonverbal messages. Much has been learned about the mechanisms involved in conveying meaning, and, at this stage of our knowledge, knowing the general origins of expressive behavior is more important than knowing the meaning of hundreds of kinemorphs. If we understand the origin of certain human behaviors, we will be better able to interpret for ourselves the actions of those with whom we interact.

Origins of nonverbal signs: nature or nurture?

A number of theories have been advanced to explain the relation between nonverbal signs and mental and physical states. Charles Darwin tendered one of the earliest explanations, arguing that human

[9] Frederick Williams and Barbara Sundene, "Dimensions of Recognition: Visual vs. Vocal Expression of Emotion," **Communication Review**, XIII (1965), 44–52.
[10] Eugene Levitt, "The Relationship between Abilities to Express Emotional Meanings Vocally and Facially," in Joel Davitz, ed., **The Communication of Emotional Meaning** (New York: McGraw-Hill Book Company, 1964), pp. 87–100.
[11] Edward Sapir, "The Unconscious Patterning of Behavior in Society," in David Mandelbaum, ed., **Selected Writings of Edward Sapir in Language, Culture and Personality** (Berkeley: University of California Press, 1949), p. 556.

expressions are remnants of the reflex responses of lower primates and primitive man. For example, in subhuman species, grinning is an expression in response to fright, a preparation to bite. But, as a modern critic of Darwin has pointed out, biting behavior has little relation to the function of grinning in human society. Man smiles when he neither verbalizes nor feels fearful or threatened.[12] Consequently, evolution may explain why an expression has found its way into man's behavioral repertoire, but it does not necessarily explain the communicative value of such an expression.

The fashion in recent years has been to attribute the meaning of expressive movement to culture. To use the terms of the familiar **nature-nurture** controversy, men do not, by nature, express themselves in a certain way, but are trained to attribute meaning to certain signs in accordance with rules specific to individual cultures. Although he carefully qualifies his position, Birdwhistell has defined the dominant opinion about the origin of expressive behavior thus: "the systematic body motion of the members of a community is considered a function of the social system to which the group belongs."[13] In this view, both verbal and nonverbal communicative systems are culture-bound and artificial. Much of the evidence points in this direction. To cite one other authority, Landis, whose work was reviewed earlier, concluded that much of man's small ability to interpret facial expression ought to be attributed to meanings assigned them by social conventions.[14] In Chapter 6 we will survey different ways various cultures signify the same meaning, and different meanings which cultures assign the same nonverbal sign. The fact that there are innumerable variations in communicative behavior among members of the world's many cultures strongly supports the case for cultural determinism. But general belief in the importance of culture in forming nonverbal codes does not rest on these differences. Rather, the argument rests squarely on the assumption that there are no universal symbols of emotional states, for if there did exist expressions of emotion which all men, regardless of culture, could use and recognize, these would have to be classified as innate or instinctual,

[12] Richard J. Andrew, "Evolution of Facial Expression," **Science,** CXLII (November 22, 1963), 1037–1039.
[13] Ray Birdwhistell, **Kinesics and Context** (Philadelphia: University of Pennsylvania Press, 1970), p. 184.
[14] Carney Landis, "Studies of Emotional Reactions," **Journal of Comparative Psychology,** IV (1924), 447–99.

just as a sound with universal meaning would be classified as innate.

Despite the great differences among the world's nonverbal codes, some evidence indicates the existence of a few universal facial expressions. Several groups of aborigines in New Guinea were asked to participate in a judgment study. The aborigines were unfamiliar with whatever conventions may exist for informing and acculturizing the subjects of western cultures. They had neither been exposed to western movies and magazines nor lived in western settlements. If they were to react to nonverbal cues in the same way as western subjects, agreement could not be explained as a result of their having learned the same stylized forms of emotional display. Each subject was shown three pictures of a face posing a different emotion, and was told a story involving only one emotion. The subject was then asked to choose the picture best illustrating the theme of the story. The results from New Guinea were then compared with scores obtained from western subjects. The correlation between the representatives of these two different cultures was high, for substantial agreement was reached for the emotions happy, sad, anger, disgust, and surprise. To confirm this finding, the aborigines were themselves asked to pose a series of emotions. Photographs of their poses were then shown to American college students who were asked to judge some of the emotional displays of a very alien society.[15] The students did rather well, thus raising serious doubts about the presumption that all modes of expression are culture-bound. Some nonverbal signs seem to be pancultural, having meaning in most or all societies.

Like most nature-nurture controversies, the debate over whether emotive sign behavior is learned or innate can be settled with gain for both sides. One possible compromise lies in an analogy between language acquisition and the acquisition of a pattern of socially usable nonverbal signs. We know that the capacity for language is innate, for all human beings display a predisposition to use a language composed of discrete sounds linked together in a structure controlled by syntactical rules. Regardless of the culture in which he is raised, a child learns to use language in the same chronological sequence as all other children. For example, he will first utter sentences at about the same age in all cultures. The same ideas may be applied to nonverbal behavior. All persons are born with the capacity to communicate with their face, hands, and eyes, and all children may learn the

[15] Ekman, Friesen, and Ellsworth, **Emotion in the Human Face.**

communicative use of their body at the same time and in the same sequence. Further, the child is born with the capacity to utter all sounds which exist in any language. Through conditioning, however, some of the sounds are not reinforced (since they are not used in the adult language) and consequently they are not repeated by the child. The same may hold true for nonverbal communication. A child born into a culture in which broad gesticulation is not general will not be reinforced when he gesticulates broadly. As a result, this particular behavior will disappear from his repertoire. From this analogy, we can draw the conclusion that the capacity for meaningful expressions is innate in human communication. Moreover, the particular symbols and signs which grow out of this capacity are culture-bound. Clearly, we shall not know whether this analogy is valid until further research is done on the acquisition of meaningful nonverbal behavior. And even if this research indicates a universal sequence, the analogy fails to explain why some signs have the same meaning in very dissimilar cultures. Another level of compromise is necessary.

The anthropologist Weston La Barre writes that "one fundamental question that needs to be investigated in kinesics is the precise boundary line between instinctual movements, expressions, and acts versus the numerous culture-based kinesic codes that must be learned like any arbitrary, invented, symbolic system."[16] This approach suggests that some expressive actions can be attributed to instinct and some to culture. A more useful way of viewing the problem is to determine the degree to which innate or learned behaviors influence the production of a given signal. Certain facial expressions, for example, may be innate in the sense that psychological and physiological processes, as they have evolved over time, determine a general human expression for an emotion. However, learned patterns control the circumstances which elicit emotion, the occasions on which certain emotions may be expressed, and the ways in which emotions may be masked. Culture, for example, determines whether a mourner should be happy or sad at a funeral, and the extent to which he can express the emotion that he has learned to feel. But the signs for happiness or sadness can be regarded as pancultural expressions.

One of the attractive aspects of a cultural theory of expression is that all meaning for movements can be explained as arbitrary inven-

---

[16] Weston La Barre, "Paralinguistics, Kinesics, and Cultural Anthropology," in Thomas Sebeok **et al.**, eds., **Approaches to Semiotics** (The Hague: Mouton, 1964), p. 194.

tions. A smile means a person is happy because he has learned a representation for happiness. The argument for innate meaning must hinge on a demonstration that certain complex universal mechanisms exist for the production and translation of emotive signs. Attitude theory and psychoanalytic theory attempt to describe such mechanisms.

Attitude theory explains universal relationships of intrapsychic state to external sign behavior. This theory originated in the reinterpretation of William James's concept that emotions are a response to action: a person feels sorry because he is crying. In attitude theory, readiness to act, and not action itself, gives rise to feeling states: we are sorry because of readiness to cry, angry because of readiness to strike and afraid because of readiness to run away. One of the leading members of this school posits that man instinctually prepares to respond to certain situations. For example, when he is threatened, an individual instinctively prepares to both attack and flee. Even though the body is prepared to act, however, such action may not be appropriate. During the period when the body is ready to act, but is prevented from doing so, emotions are generated. Thus, feelings are explained as secondary to and dependent upon bodily preparation for action maintained in a preliminary stage of readiness. Two important experiments were conducted to support this theory. The purpose of the first was to discover if there was a relationship between emotion and postural set. Subjects were hypnotized and told to feel certain emotions, and for every emotion, each subject assumed approximately the same postural set. But, the researcher wanted to know, how intimately are posture and emotion related? A second experiment was conducted to see if emotion could change without postural change. Subjects were again hypnotized and told to feel a particular emotion and to assume the postural set appropriate to it. They were then instructed to hold the same posture but to feel an opposite emotion. It was found that no new feeling state came into being when posture was not changed. On the basis of these experiments, one researcher concluded that "there is a functional and irreversible relationship between the body attitude, with its musculoskeletal, visceral, vascular and glandular components, and the feeling, or 'affective' part of consciousness."[17] One of the ways you can verify

[17] Nina Bull, **The Body and Its Mind** (New York: Las Americas, 1962), pp. 17–39.

this hypothesis for yourself is to assume a body attitude which indicates emotions that are the opposite of those you feel. Suppose that you feel depressed. Will walking with a firm stride, head upright and chest out change the way you feel? Returning to the debate over the origin of nonverbal signs, we suggest that attitude theory supports the conclusion that, because of similar physical construction and common instinctual drives, all men feel approximately the same emotions and express them nonverbally in approximately the same way.

Classical **psychoanalytic theory** posits the reverse of attitude theory: similar psychological mechanisms operating on the body produce universal forms for the expression of feeling. Psychoanalysts are principally concerned with the way in which the body manifests psychic experience. On the most superficial level, they presuppose the existence of mind-body connections which those familiar with psychoanalytic dogma might easily predict. Why, for example, does a speaker cough, or drink water, or clean his glasses while he talks? "Such mannerisms are a denial of danger; they are a clinging to inanimate things since the other person, the mother, is not available."[18] Going further in the same direction, another analyst, William Needles, sees nonverbal communication as regressive behavior. He notes that patients vary greatly in the degree to which they gesticulate. For example, the person who saws the air with his hand is seeking an outlet for his emotions which even vehement speech will not afford. For some psychiatrists, "gesticulation, as an accompaniment, or substitute for, speech, bears all the ear-marks of regressive behavior."[19] Felix Deutsch, discussing posture rather than gesture, argues that the mind uses the body to release anxiety. On the most general level, he asserts that "there are definite motivations for the postural behavior of every patient. Postural attitudes reflect or substitute, precede or accompany the verbal expression of unconscious material."[20] All patients have characteristic postures which change when the need arises to express or repress an anxiety. Changes of posture are thus tension-releasing mechanisms. Whether the explanation for kinesic and postural behavior involves regressive behavior,

[18] S. S. Feldman, "Mannerisms of Speech: A Contribution to the Working Through Process," **Psychoanalytic Quarterly**, XVII (1948), 367.
[19] William Needles, "Gesticulation and Speech," **International Journal of Psychoanalysis**, XL (1959), 291.
[20] Felix Deutsch, "Analysis of Postural Behavior," **Psychoanalytic Quarterly**, XVI (1947), 211.

clinging to a love object, or more general tension release, psycho-analysts agree that there is an integral relationship between mind and body. Specific connections which apply to all men who are engaged in nonverbal communication cannot be easily drawn, however, since the psychodynamics which analysts describe may be peculiar to western culture. Future observation should be directed toward discovering if common mental operations produce common physiological manifestations.

Summary

In this chapter we have sought the meaning of nonverbal signs in the link between emotion and behavior. Our search has led to two ways of understanding expressive movement. One attributes meaning to the same cultural learning that accounts for meaning in language, and the other focuses on the innate meaning of certain signs. In accounting for nonverbal meaning, we have relied on systematic observation of human behavior. And in accounting for the mechanisms which supply sense to human communicative action, we shall now move beyond this behavioral approach to an analysis of the psychosomatic dynamics of expression.

FOUR

Nonverbal meaning: a physiological approach

The body as medium

The transmission of meaning from one organism to another is inextricably bound up with the physical structure and function of the communicators. One cannot fully understand a message without understanding the body which is its medium. For example, as one writer has noted,

> postures and movements communicate at best something generally about tension and tension-release. Without additional information, one could make no clear distinction therefore between, say, stiffness due to brain tumor, military training, rheumatism, hostility, meningitis, etc.[1]

When we assess body signs, our attempt to infer meaning without knowledge of organic processes can lead to painfully wrong conclusions. Unfortunately, an increased understanding of the physiology of nonverbal communication is not a major goal of current research. A comment written a number of years ago still holds true:

> An analysis of our current thinking will show that it tends to suffer

[1] Peter Ostwald, "How the Patient Communicates about Disease with the Doctor," in Thomas Sebeok et al., eds., **Approaches to Semiotics** (The Hague: Mouton, 1964), p. 15.

47

generally from a failure to view mental activities in their proper relation,
or even in any relation, to motor behavior.[2]

Students of human behavior have long been confused by the relationship of mental activities to the physical structure of the neuro-
muscular system. Nineteenth-century religious orthodoxy dictated the
notion that man thinks, feels, and remembers because of the operation of an immaterial mind or soul upon a material brain. Phrenologists
elaborated this theory by drawing functional charts of the brain. One
area was assigned responsibility for the feelings of love, another for
the ability to engage in abstract reasoning, and so on until each category of human feeling had been given a physical site. Although
phrenological theory is backed by precious little evidence, it attracted
adherents because it provided an easily comprehensible anatomical
explanation for human behavior. Why were some individuals brilliant
analysts and, at the same time, emotional imbeciles? Because their
forebrains were well developed and their hindbrains were shriveled.
Phrenology was forgotten by the early twentieth century, except in
such phrases as "highbrow." Psychologists began to speak of drives
or instincts, presumably enmeshed in the circuitry of the cortex, in
their theories of human action. Instincts to love, or to dominate, or to
fight were used to explain loving, power-seeking, and fighting. Such
theorizing was soon abandoned, largely because of its circularity.
Any observed set of behaviors could be explained as the product of a
newly invented drive.

Using as a model the physical sciences with their emphasis on
"hard" data, psychologists turned to two kinds of study. The first kind
focused on the mechanisms of human behavior. Physiological psychologists carefully dissected animal and human specimens, examining neurons and their terminal arborizations. They bombarded subjects with hosts of stimuli, searching for clues to the physiological
process of perception. Unfortunately, the data generated by these
studies lacked applicability to the more interesting questions about
human behavior. Threshold responses to pain were discovered, but
insights into why men inflicted pain upon one another were not.

The second kind of study emphasized the systematic observation
of behavior, usually under controlled circumstances. The reasoning

[2] R. W. Sperry, "Neurology and Mid-Brain Problem," **American Scientist,** XL
(1952), 291–312.

justifying this effort is much the same one might use in learning to operate a computer. Suppose you were at a computer's control console. In front of you is a blank television screen and in the corner is a bank of interconnecting circuits. Your job is to explain the operation of the machine. (Your predecessor, a fussy electrician, thought he could explain how the machine worked by tracing the circuitry in the wiring bank. All began well enough for him, but soon the circuits became so complex and the relays so tiny that he began to report things like "the red wire leads to the blue wire which leads to the green wire." After a few years of this drivel, his employers retired him.) Attempting to find a different approach, you push buttons at random, and the screen lights up. As you push more buttons, you find that by hitting the 2 button and the "add" button, the screen starts flashing 2-4-6-8. After several years of this random discovery, you will have compiled a lengthy log of what the machine will do when a particular set of buttons is pushed. But does this really explain how the machine operates? Yes, in the sense that the log shows what inputs (buttons pushed) produce what outputs (flashes on the screen). You have shown how to operate the machine, and no further knowledge about the bank of wires would improve the performance of future operators. Like the electrician, physiological psychologists have attempted to explain the operation of the human machine by studying the wiring. However, behaviorists are interested in which buttons produce which results, not in the operations which lie in between.

To take the computer analogy just one step further, the electrician and the button-pusher can help one another. The button-pusher can control the machine, but he cannot improve upon its operation. The electrician can indicate to him what happens when he puts something into the circuitry, although he has no concept of what causes certain currents to pass through his wiring. Thus, the button-pusher can describe the larger purposes of the machine. Chapter 3, with the exception of the references to psychoanalytic and attitude theory, was based on data obtained from the button-pushers. In this chapter, we will deal with the electrician's data. Less metaphorically, the first part of this chapter will summarize that portion of anatomical and physiological knowledge which helps to explain the organic processes involved in the communication of meaning. Physiologists cannot, of course, fully explain every event which lies between the reception of a stimulus and the observable response to it. There is a level of thought processes at which physical evidence explains little. Once we are at that level, we must revert to a model based on inferences about what must happen for certain behaviors to occur. The presentation of this model will take up the second part of this chapter.

Before discussing either organic data or thought process models, the three levels of analysis which we have designated—external behavior, organic processes, and inferred mental operation—should be placed in proper perspective. Figure 4–1 indicates a relationship

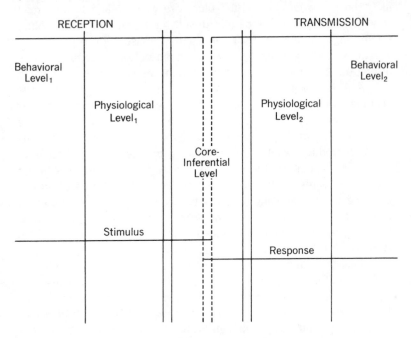

Figure 4–1

between them. Notice that the diagram has two main parts, labeled "reception" and "transmission." Both these processes can be analyzed on behavioral, physiological, and thought process levels. The first behavioral level involves the reception of stimuli. As an example, let's say that the stimulus is the pressure of someone's foot on your big toe. This can be described physiologically by tracing the path of a nerve impulse from pressure receptors in the toe to the brain. Your reaction to this nerve impulse will be mediated through mental processes which cannot be physically traced. The reaction itself, however, can be followed as an increase of adrenalin triggering the dilation of blood vessels, which appears externally as a flushed face. Each of the three levels of analysis, then, must be considered to give a complete answer to the question, "Why did your face become flushed when someone stepped on your big toe?"

Our primary objective in this chapter is to explain what happens in individuals when they interact with one another. As we investigate the intrapersonal mechanisms of nonverbal communication, we also wish to return to the central question presented in the last chapter: How do cultural patterns and innate human traits influence communication behavior? Edward Hall articulates well a general view of their relationship. He refers to the

> physiological base shared by all human beings, to which culture gives structure and meaning. It is this **pre**cultural sensory base to which the scientist must inevitably refer in comparing the proxemic [and other nonverbal] patterns of Culture A with those of Culture B.[3]

The connections between cultural and precultural elements can best be understood by examining the intrapersonal process involved in the act of sending messages. The individual as communicator must be able to receive and transmit data, relate and store information, and perform complex acts of thought. For each process, somatic and cultural forces stand in different relations of importance to one another.

The physiology of stimulus reception

Human beings receive sensory impressions through organs of vision, hearing, taste, touch, and smell. These organs consist of highly specialized nerve endings which connect with the brain by way of the nervous system. The physical structure of these sense organs plays an important role in the determination of communicative behavior in several ways. First, the degree to which each type of organ relies on different message systems is determined by the amount of data which the organ can receive from the environment and send to the brain. The eye can gather more information over a far greater distance than the ear, and the ear in turn can gather more information than chemo-

---

[3] Edward Hall, **Hidden Dimension** (Garden City, N.Y.: Doubleday & Company, Inc., 1966), p. 101.

ceptors in the nose or pressure receptors in the skin. Thus, the complexity of structure and function of each organ, and the manner in which organs are neurally linked to the brain, are major determinants of the amount of sense data each organ can collect. In the context of nonverbal communication, the eye can scan for many different and subtle signals, the ear fewer, and the skin fewest. As a result, one would expect visual cues to be most important in nonverbal communication and sound cues less important. Indeed, except with regard to lovemaking and the blind, we rarely think of the sense of touch as being involved in human interaction. However, even though physiology may establish some general rank order among different kinds of nonverbal messages, culture also plays a role. For example, in some human groups, the sense of smell is granted a higher priority than in others. Thus, the structure of the body establishes a propensity to use certain signal systems, but, within the order thus created, culture also generates variations.

Second, physiology also shapes the specific messages which individuals send one another. The distance between individuals who are interacting is partially determined by the physical structure of sense receptors. For example, acuity of vision is greatest in the center of the field of focus because one area of the retina of the eye, the fovea, is richly endowed with nerve endings. When two people stand close to one another, they can bring into sharp focus only a small part of each other's face. At longer distances, a larger part of the other person can be clearly seen until the distance is increased so greatly that finer features can no longer be distinguished. Thus, how people space themselves is influenced by what the fovea allows them to see clearly. The potential sensitivity of chemoceptors and thermoreceptors plays a part parallel to that of the fovea in controlling proxemic patterns. Only within certain distances does a human being receive a sufficient kind and concentration of molecules from his conversational partner to actually smell him. Similarly, only within a certain distance can we feel the body heat of another. Again, however, culture meshes with physiology to control behavior. What we wish to see, smell, and feel of others are learned preferences.

If a man were fully conscious of the infinite number of stimuli to which he is daily exposed, he would probably die. The consequences can be compared to overloading an electric circuit. Part of the job of screening stimuli is performed by the receptor end-organs themselves. Specialized receptor cells possess thresholds of excitation such that in order for them to be stimulated, the incoming signals must be of a given intensity and duration. So much light or so much pressure is needed to fire a neuron in the eye or the skin, although the exact amount of stimulation needed varies from individual to individual. Insensibility to nonverbal cues, then, can be attributed in some instances to organic factors. Examples are: (1) the threshold levels of neural excitability are dependent upon such factors as the amounts of oxygen, carbon dioxide, calcium, and potassium in the blood; (2) the extent of general fatigue influences the excitability of nerve endings; and (3) overbombardment of a particular organ reduces excitability. Because of these factors, the same individual may vary in his receptivity to nonverbal cues over the course of his lifetime, or even during a single day.

Man can be deprived of his senses either wholly or partially. An individual who loses his sight or his hearing is unable to participate in a whole range of nonverbal communication. Fortunately, more and more means for increasing the use of substitute sense modalities are being explored. In addition to the traditional aids such as braille reading, researchers have built highly sophisticated instruments to more directly change visual cues into pressure cues, and have explored the possibility of using vibratory sensations to transmit words to the mind through the skin.[4] Since partial blocking of sensory reception is perhaps more common than total loss, ways to heighten muted perception can be fairly effective. In analyzing individual participation in nonverbal interaction, we can attribute partial inability to receive signals to some extent to physical disability and in some cases to preventable causes such as malnutrition, drugs, and intense noise levels.

Except when we feel pain, most of us are unaware of internal sense receptors. Yet the stimuli which originate within the body, and which are received by sense organs called **interoceptors,** are just as important for existence and for communication as the external sensory apparatus. Interoceptors are liberally distributed throughout various tissues and organs. If you were to close your eyes and raise your arm above your head, you would know the position of the arm because of the existence of a special kind of interoceptor called a **proprioceptor.**

[4] Frank A. Geldard, "Bod'y Eng'lish," **Psychology Today,** II (December 1968), 43–47.

The individual is unaware of a great deal of information which interoceptors dispatch to the brain. At this moment, you might be wholly unconscious of your heartbeat, or the location of your right big toe. Even these unconscious data are used by the brain to coordinate systemic organ function. Of importance to the communication process is the role of interoception in self-feedback. When an individual speaks, he hears himself and he also feels what is happening to his jaw. Thus, he receives several types of information about the same act. His redundant nervous system is constantly monitoring what is happening inside and outside the body. This is important for participation in a nonverbal communication situation. We learn from our culture such phrases as, "She blushed with embarrassment," or, "He trembled with rage." Within specific contexts, learned formulae such as these might be sufficient to allow us to ascribe meaning to reactions. But we also know how others feel on the basis of their nonverbal behaviors because, in contact with ourselves through the interoceptive system, we associate certain acts and body sensations with particular emotions. We know embarrassment as a flushed face, and so, when someone else blushes, we are ready to assume that he feels as we have felt.

Mental processes and nonverbal communication

Sensory inputs are essential for the normal functioning of the thought process. As one psychologist has written, "the restriction of sensory input from the exteroceptors would be expected to disrupt thinking and the adequacy of cognitive and visual motor performance."[5] The way in which information is conveyed from the nerve ending to the brain, while generally understood, is still the subject of debate. Until recently, it was believed that particular nerves leading from the sense organs to the brain carried qualitatively different signals, and "different qualities of sensation, such as pain, taste, and color, along with other mental attributes, might be correlated with the discharge of specific modes of nervous energy."[6] Although some evidence supports this view, current belief holds that all nerve impulses are alike. Impulses traveling over the optic, auditory, and other sensory

[5] John Zubeck, **Sensory Deprivation: Fifteen Years of Research** (New York: Appleton-Century-Crofts, 1969), p. 415.
[6] E. Herring, **Memory: Lectures on the Specific Energies of the Nervous System.** (Chicago: Open Court, 1913).

nerves are similar in nature.[7] We feel different sensations because the nerves terminate in different parts of the brain. The parts of the brain responsible for decoding nonverbal signals, in one opinion, are the "phylogenetically old structures of the central and autonomic nervous systems."[8]

Despite what is known about the structure of the brain, the most practical way of discussing mental events is to conceptualize the processes which must occur rather than tracing the pathways of individual neural impulses. Thought processes can be described and related to one another in the form of a model, a verbal picture of what probably happens when a set of inputs is transformed into a particular set of outputs. The model which we have adopted for picturing thought processes involved in communication is one worked out by Wiseman and Barker (see Figure 4–2).[9] Each of the designations in this model represents a process which logically must be a part of the total act

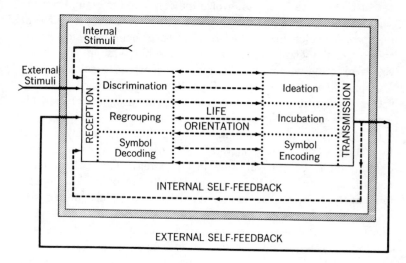

Figure 4–2

[7] R. W. Sperry, "Mechanisms of Neural Maturation," in S. S. Stevens, ed., **Handbook of Experimental Psychology** (New York: John Wiley & Sons, Inc., 1951), pp. 273–74.
[8] Jurgen Ruesch, "Nonverbal Language," in Robert Cathcart and Larry Samovar, eds., **Small Group Communication** (Dubuque: Brown, 1970), p. 262.
[9] Larry Barker and Gordon Wiseman, "A Model of Intrapersonal Communication," **Journal of Communication**, XVI (1966), 174. Reprinted by permission.

of communication. The position of each designation on the diagram is a rough specification of a temporal sequence of mental events which occur within the communicator. The processes move from left to right. In the next few pages, we shall examine the probable nature of mental events by using the key terms of this model.

Discrimination. Man cannot be sensitive to all the stimuli which are within his range of receptivity. The mind must be able to honor certain stimuli and reject others. While you are reading this book, a dozen or more stimuli are doubtless being picked up by your sense receptors: street noise, the temperature of the air, the ache in your back, and the like. In order to concentrate on the visual stimulation of this book, you must screen out other sensations. What you exclude from consciousness is partly a matter of physiological design, but people do have options as to which stimuli they will recognize. For example, activity concerned with heart action is not consciously perceived because it fails to involve the cortex of the brain. However, when you listen to a speaker, you can either perceive the sound of the speaker's voice, the sight of the light waves being reflected off the speaker, or the vibrations of the air-conditioning system. The choice you take, as the Wiseman-Barker model suggests, is predicated upon your particular life experience. Does that life experience condition you to think that the speaker's words are more important than his appearance, or that neither is of any consequence?

Differences in discrimination among people are largely derived from culture. Each culture imprints upon its young a series of patterns of attention having survival value. In Japan, for instance, children are conditioned from birth to tolerate extremely hot baths. The inhabitants of North Africa can stand motionless, their bodies covered with small flies and insects, impervious to the presence of these tiny poachers. Most Americans would find a Japanese bath at least uncomfortably warm, and would not fail to notice that a fly had landed on their skin. Variations among groups in what is noticed are not determined by genetic differences in sensory receptors, but by what a culture has taught its members is worth noticing.

The discriminatory process is quite important for nonverbal communication. We are physiologically incapable of monitoring simultaneously everything we do with our bodies. Consequently, we do not notice all the meaningful cues we send to others, and further, we cannot possibly take in all the stimuli sent to us by others. As a result, individuals are trained to be sensitive to a few of the many available sources of information about others. One might hazard the guess that Americans discriminate against touch and smell signals in preference to sight, sound, and taste signals. This statement must be modified, however, since the members of any one culture will differ in their discriminatory procedures because they have, in the course of their lives, learned the unstated rules of their culture somewhat differently.

Regrouping. Regrouping is a process by which the vast amounts of raw data entering the body are sorted into meaningful patterns. Sense impressions are, after all, only a mélange of reactions to light, sound, and the like. How do we know that the brown, pink, and yellow light wave frequencies fit together to form a human being? The answer rests in our innate ability to group together these various stimuli. Thus, physiological patterns, in the sense of a neurological grid, may account for some aspects of the regrouping process. (When chemicals such as LSD are introduced into the brain, they can change this neurological pattern, allowing a revised ordering of stimuli perception.) Individuals also learn how to group certain stimuli in the course of their lives. In nonverbal communication, the selective groupings which an individual makes are essential for his comprehension of incoming messages. Through grouping, he can link together diverse kinds of stimuli into potentially meaningful patterns.

Symbol decoding. Meaning must be supplied to those stimulus patterns about which men consciously think. Wiseman and Barker apparently assume that we supply such meaning symbols only during the process of communication. We know that verbal discourse and sign language, made up of symbols which stand for or refer to something else, have a special kind of meaning which must be decoded by the use of a language key. Moreover, the signs which make up much nonverbal discourse also have to be interpreted. We have said a great deal about this process of interpretation earlier in the discussion of perception. Here, however, we will simply point out that no intelligent response to stimuli is possible unless the stimuli are first supplied with meaning.

Some nonverbal cues are interpreted in the same way as verbal cues. Such interpretation is learned by mastering a given culture's system of arbitrary meaning. Decoding also occurs through the empathic recognition of common feelings mentioned earlier in our discussion of interoception. In addition, certain processes of inference facilitate decoding. Paul Secord has briefly outlined some of these processes for the attribution of meaning. His concepts were developed with special reference to facial expression, but several of the inferential processes which he mentions have wider application to all expressive signs. First, perceivers of another person define that person's personality by seizing on a momentary expression—a frown means that he is sad. Second, a perceiver transfers what he has learned about the nonverbal signs associated with one person to another person. Throughout life, we build upon experience with others a kind of nonverbal glossary which is quite effective if all the people we are likely to meet are the same. But when we communicate with individuals from different cultural backgrounds, such previous learning can betray us into misreading nonverbal cues. Third, on the basis of outward signs, perceivers categorize people, and then add certain characteristics to these categories. When we hear a southern drawl, we categorize the speaker, assuming that he has certain attitudes toward race, and act toward him as if he does. Last, we make generalizations based on figurative analogies.[10] For example, the meaning attributed to a strong handshake may be that the shaker has a strong personality. These, then, are some of the possible ways meaning is attributed to action, ways nonverbal signals are deciphered.

Life orientation, ideation, and incubation. These three terms designate the central processes of thought. They refer generally to the totality of ways man views the world, analyzes it, and stores his analyses until action is appropriate. On these vague terms, or ones like them, philosophers have sought to hang innumerable concepts about the operation of man's mind. However, the concepts themselves remain indistinct. In relation to nonverbal communication, life orientation influences, as Figure 4–2 suggests, each of the other processes. Ideation is, again, a concept arising from a definition of communication which is oriented toward verbal expression. Many of the signals which men send do not arise from what would normally be called thought, but from habit. Therefore, the third concept, incubation, is relevant since many of our actions are held in abeyance because they are not defined by us as appropriate for the communication situation.

---

[10] Paul F. Secord, "Facial Features and Inference Processes in Interpersonal Perception," in Renato Tagiuri and Luigi Petrullo, eds., **Person Perception and Interpersonal Behavior** (Stanford: Stanford University Press, 1958), pp. 313–314.

Symbol encoding and transmission. Thoughts and feelings are often put into understandable form through symbolization which occurs on the cortical level. But only a small proportion of thoughts find expression in verbal or iconic form. The greater proportion are retained internally and are either stored in a memory bank or expressed in some motoric behavior. At this point, we can leave the conceptualizations of the model and return to what is known about the physiology of expressive behavior.

Any individual movement is a complex physical process. As one investigator pointed out,

> the simple act of [one's] raising his hand to his mouth to stifle a yawn requires the transmission from the brain of precisely related electric control signals to synchronize the contraction of 58 different muscles working on 32 separate bones in the hand and arm, not to mention the considerable fraction of the 31 muscles of the face that move the features and produce its various expressions.[11]

Nonverbal transmission, then, involves a high level of motoric activity.

Many human expressions are transmitted intrapersonally—the message begins and ends within the same body. One physician refers to the fact that

> emotional feelings, instead of finding expression and discharge in the symbolic use of words and appropriate behavior, must be conceived as being translated into a kind of "organ language."[12]

While you were making a speech, you may have noticed a queasy feeling in your stomach. Such feelings of nervousness, or indeed, of excitement and elation, are caused by the transmission of specific neural impulses to particular glands, organs, and tissues.

Many intrapersonal communications can only be detected by experts using sophisticated instruments. The physician is on constant alert for such cues which, when decoded, help him make a diagnosis. Headaches, high blood pressure, gastrointestinal abnormalities may all indicate something about the condition of the patient. Lie detectors are also used for tuning-in on the intrapersonal communication network. The body transmits data to the machine through changes in

---

[11] Dean Wooldridge, **The Machinery of the Brain** (New York: McGraw-Hill Book Company, 1963), p. 62.
[12] Paul MacLean, "Psychosomatic Disease and the Visceral Brain," **Psychosomatic Medicine**, XI (1949), 347.

blood pressure, breathing, pulse, and electrical potential of the skin.

Some manifestations of intrapersonal communication are obvious to the nonexpert, and form an important class of nonverbal displays. One writer has described the skin as a

> kind of advertising bill-board that broadcasts to the world what goes on under its surface. · . . . By means of pilo-erection, vasomotor change, pigmentation, exudation, and other signs, the skin also transmits information about the bearer's emotions. Fear gives him goosepimples and pallor, anger produces flushing and mottling. . . .[13]

Thus, individuals transmit their feelings to others in the course of carrying on biologically essential activity, or inadvertently through nonconscious intrapersonal communication. This kind of signaling is the nonverbal activity which is least likely to be influenced by cultural prescription.

The learning of habit patterns through imitation of others is the last form of motoric activity with which we are concerned. These patterns of motor discharge are highly complex. Consider the extraordinary coordination required to say a simple sentence. Vocal cords, lungs, hands, neck muscles, etc., must all be activated in concert at the right moment. The habits allowing such a performance are learned in the culture. However, breakdowns in communicational coordination can be caused by neurological and muscular disorders.

Long-established patterns of movement can, moreover, alter the musculature of the body, and body expression can thus become quite physically inflexible. If an individual continually expresses himself in the same way,

> the muscular arrangement becomes set. Materially speaking some muscles shorten and thicken, others are invaded by connective tissues. . . . Once this has happened the body attitude is invariable; it is involuntary; it can no longer be changed basically by taking thought or even by mental suggestion.[14]

Even socially learned habits, then, can become physiologically fixed.

Summary

In this and the preceding chapter, we have taken a look at the individual communicator: specifically how he transmits and decodes signals.

[13] Ostwald, "How the Patient Communicates about Disease," p. 13.
[14] Ida Rolf, "Structural Integration," **Systematics,** I (1963), 72.

Our concern, in the main, has been with the question of meaning. To what degree is nonverbal meaning arbitrary and to what degree is it innate? How do individuals reveal their feelings, and how are these feelings interpreted by others?

Ultimately, a human being is a system within a system, for the larger world of interaction in which he is immersed is governed by social purposes and rules which must be understood if we are to account for the meaning of nonverbal signs.

FIVE

Social functions
of nonverbal communication

Nonverbal cues serve social purposes. Like verbal symbols, they convey information and facilitate the integration of human action and feeling. This generalization applies to all societies. For even though specific meanings attributed to some actions may vary dramatically from culture to culture, nonverbal messages universally serve informational and integrative purposes. This chapter is an overview of the general functions served by expressive behavior; the following two chapters will examine nonverbal communication in cultural contexts.

Transmission of information

When people talk, they can use language to discuss anything for which they possess shared symbols. While conversation may be about such abstract matters as the nature of God or the condition of the economy, the nonverbal cues expressed during conversation principally provide data about the individuals themselves. Words may also carry this sort of information, since people can choose to talk about their characteristics, motives, and feelings. But, for reasons to be discussed later, we place great reliance on nonverbal channels for critical information about the other fellow. The social psychologist Anselm Strauss, analyzing the exchange of information during social interaction, writes that each person involved must be alert to a myriad of cues to determine three things:

> (1) the other's general intent in the situation; (2) the other's response toward himself; and (3) the other's response or feeling toward me, the recipient of his action.[1]

What does a stranger want, is he sure of himself, and will he do me harm? These are the kinds of questions which occur during an initial encounter. Part of this information is provided by the context in which the encounter occurs—we impute characteristics to another because he is in a certain place at a particular time. A student generally knows how others will react to him in a classroom, a bar, or the cafeteria, and he structures his behavior to cope with these expected reactions. We can also draw inferences from the words chosen to convey a message. When you ask another individual for the time, a response of, "Sorry, I don't have a watch," or, "What's it to yeh, Mac," tells much about the other person's intent, self-evaluation, and attitude toward you. Of course, information arising from the context and the verbal message is supplemented by information conveyed by voice, appearance, and action.

Giving and gleaning information is not restricted to the initial phases of an interaction. Every word or action may modify the intent and attitudes of each interactant. The first few minutes of many meetings are devoted to friendly banter. Then, one or two significant participants decide that serious discussion should begin. Subtle cues indicate their shift of purpose: a change of expression, tone of voice, or body posture. Recognition of these cues facilitates a smooth transition from one phase of the meeting to another, whereas failure to notice such signs leaves members of the group acting at cross-purposes.

People often emit signals indicating that, during the course of an interaction, their feelings about themselves have changed. An individual whose suggestions are ignored in a small group may become angry, apathetic, or withdrawn. Whichever occurs, his self-image in relation to the group changes as manifested by shifts of body and facial expression and denunciatory or self-deprecating words, or a

[1] Anselm Strauss, **Mirrors and Masks: The Search for Identity** (New York: The Free Press, 1956), p. 59.

failure to speak at all. The member who feels slighted by others often turns his entire body away from the center of the group, refuses to make eye contact, and holds his face immobile in a neutral or pained expression. If the rest of the group is oblivious to these signals, an alienated member can eventually demoralize or disrupt the entire group.

On the basis of what we say, other individuals can quickly change their opinion of us. The effective group member or public speaker constantly surveys his auditors to judge their reaction to him and his ideas. Even a group or audience that appears to be relatively passive sends many messages about their degree of involvement and acceptance of what is being said. Failure to look at the speaker, small nervous gestures, an overly relaxed posture, can all signal boredom. Novice speakers are sometimes told to create the illusion that they are looking at their audience by staring directly at the wall in back of the room. Although such advice may be helpful for some—and indicates a cultural norm which requires eye contact—it prevents the speaker from carefully watching the audience to gauge effects and, if necessary, to change strategy to gain greater impact. Speakers sometimes impose similarly misguided requirements upon their audiences, such as not to engage in behavior which signals lack of interest or acceptance. Elementary school teachers are perhaps the worst such offenders, since they are in the somewhat unique position (for a speaker) of having a great deal of formal power over the behavior of their auditors. Consequently, many teachers punish students who continually look out the window—a sign of boredom—rather than attempting to communicate something which will interest the child.

Integration of action and feelings

We watch, and otherwise monitor the behavior of others, in order to decide how we should behave to achieve a desired effect. Michael Argyle, a British social psychologist, phrases this idea succinctly:

> Subject **A** will have his own characteristic set of social techniques, but these will vary to some extent according to the age, sex and personality of the other, of **B**. **A** will use one set of techniques for one group of people, and a somewhat different set for another group. Before he can select one style rather than another, **A** has to perceive and categorize **B**.[2]

[2] Michael Argyle, **The Psychology of Interpersonal Behavior** (Baltimore: Penguin Books, 1967), p. 46.

Almost everyone behaves differently toward different kinds of people. For example, a man may be brusque with his subordinates, ingratiating to his superiors, and tender with his family.

Some of the categories which people use to guide their communicative behavior are established by social structure. In American society, the rich, middle-income, and poor, the educated and uneducated, blacks and whites are treated differently. Individuals, influenced by their own characteristics and life experience, personality, and goals, modify general social categories through interpretation, elaboration, and addition. One group of researchers found that subjects who were asked to give "free descriptions" of other people tend to apply a few broad categories to very different kinds of people. Interestingly, the subjects also apply these few categories in reference to themselves.[3] How people build individual systems of categorization can be seen in a young child's behavior. He may extend treatment to others according to accepted age categories, but he adds precise gradations for those between one and five, five and seven, and seven to ten, lumping everyone over fourteen into one blurred adult concept. Union representatives who must elaborate categories, divide blue-collar workers into the organized and the unorganized. And while the general public classifies any college graduate as educated, college professors often see clear gradations between those with bachelors', masters', and doctoral degrees. When people make categories which have no general social significance, they sometimes apply the maxim, "To the man who has a toothache, all the world is a tooth." Shoe salesmen may divide the world into those people who want shoes and those who do not, and dog owners separate the world into dog- and nondog-loving people. Of course, individuals can shrink the number of categories which are accepted in the society at large. For example, the most important variable in a provincial person's communicative behavior may be whether he is talking to a local resident or to an outsider.

Categorization can proceed in subtle ways involving nonverbal signals. Salesmen adjust their spiels to fit the customer who signals either suspicion or parsimony. Speakers can detect from the general demeanor of their auditors those who are hostile and those who are friendly. A popular writer on nonverbal communication asserts that the sexually sophisticated can recognize a "potential bed-partner" at

[3] Albert Hastorf **et al.,** "The Problem of Relevance in the Study of Person Perception," in Renato Tagiuri and Luigi Petrullo, eds., **Person Perception and Interpersonal Behavior** (Stanford: Stanford University Press, 1958), pp. 54–62.

a glance.[4] Classification also depends upon the emotional state of the other person, and nonverbal cues provide this information.

Each individual should ideally be judged on his own merits, and we should always be "ourselves." Still, all people impose categories on the world, and all of us have set routines by which we respond to others. If communication is to be satisfying for the participants, individual systems of classification and individual repertoires of behavior must be consonant enough with reality to allow for the coordination of social techniques. Argyle writes that

> If **A**'s and **B**'s techniques are not coordinated, neither set of techniques will be successful; particularly in relation to affiliative needs the experience of clashing techniques is felt immediately to be jarring and unpleasant.[5]

Argyle lists seven dimensions along which individuals must synchronize their behavior: amount of speech; the speed or tempo of interaction; dominance; intimacy; cooperation and competition; emotional tone; and task, topic, and procedure. Several of these dimensions refer largely to nonverbal expression. The tempo of interaction depends upon the rate of speech, shortness of interval between replies, and the rate of movement of eyes, facial muscles, and body. Intimacy is communicated by close physical proximity and constant eye contact, as well as by words. The emotional tone of the participants is signalled by face and body.[6] Thus, if communication is to proceed smoothly, at least some of the participants must coordinate their behavior by employing nonverbal cues as their guide. And this monitoring must be used with caution to insure that others are not bridling at the techniques being used on them.

Communication and social identity

Implicit in what we have just said is the idea that each person's psychic well-being depends upon manipulating the image which he presents to others. That is, the individual's definition of himself is shaped and sustained by the reaction of other people to him. If the individual cannot elicit predictable reactions to his self-presentation,

[4] Julius Fast, **Body Language** (New York: Evans, 1970), pp. 11–13.
[5] Argyle, **The Psychology of Interpersonal Behavior,** p. 51.
[6] **Ibid.,** pp. 52–54.

then he cannot maintain a stable and consistent image of himself. Ernest Becker, an eclectic social scientist, rightly argues that the purpose of social conventions about interaction is to protect man's fragile sense of self-esteem, the human device for protecting the psyche from overwhelming anxiety. Since the sense of self is created through interaction with others, self-validation is only possible through meaningful action in a social context. Nor is the creation of a self ever completed. In the continuing process of interaction, the sense of self is modified. However, the very social intercourse which gives birth to self also threatens it. "In the social encounter each member exposes for public scrutiny and possible undermining, the one thing he needs most: the positive self-evaluation he has so laboriously fashioned." To protect the self from destruction by others, every society informally legislates rules predicated upon the enjoinder, "Let us all protect each other so that we can carry on the business of living."[7]

The most incisive recent analysis of interaction ritual for the maintenance of self has been made by the sociologist Erving Goffman who has studied the connection between information-giving and the protection of identity. He contends that "there is a relation here between informational terms and ritual ones. Failure to regulate the information acquired by the audience involves possible disruption of the situation. . . ."[8] Only by presenting the information appropriate to the situation can the individual guard his sense of worth.

When we learn about others, we place varying degrees of reliance on different kinds of behavior. As a general rule, we give greatest weight to those aspects of expressive behavior over which the individual has, ostensibly, little or no control. As Goffman puts it, "others are likely to check up on the more controllable aspects of behavior by means of the less controllable."[9] Individuals can easily fake their identities or their emotions by using false verbal statements. We know that others can forge their credentials partly because all of us, to a greater or lesser extent, have ourselves made false claims about our backgrounds or proficiency. Facial expression is somewhat less amenable to manipulation, but Paul Ekman has con-

[7] Ernest Becker, **The Birth and Death of Meaning** (New York: The Free Press, 1962), pp. 94, 108.
[8] Erving Goffman, **The Presentation of Self in Everyday Life** (Garden City, N.Y.: Doubleday Anchor Books, 1959), p. 67.
[9] **Ibid.,** p. 7.

cluded that the face is the most facile nonverbal liar.[10] The more per-
manent the habit, the more remote from conscious control, the more
it clearly indicates accurate data. People smile nearly at will, but
blush only in uncontrollable embarrassment.

Self-protection through self-control

To be able to control the usually uncontrollable aspects of his performance is, of course, to a person's advantage. Such control is the
way a con-artist or a professional actor lives and is, perhaps, a crucial
element in all social interaction. Goffman argues that every individual's behavior can be analyzed in dramatistic terms, as a stage
performance managed through exquisite control of many aspects of
behavior and environment. Before making a speech, one usually plans
the behavior which will bring forth a favorable response. In fact, books
propose rules for acting the role of the speaker: "hold hands loosely
at your sides," "don't lean back and forth," and the like. Less formal
communication situations are covered by etiquette books. But, in the
main, proper acting is learned through imitation and the implicit in-
structions constantly given during the course of childhood socialization.

Social rules are not designed to uncover frauds, but to give and
protect valid identities by defending the individual's performance.
The performance itself is guided by clusters of behavioral prescriptions which guide role portrayal. An individual learns a role when he
finds out what others expect him to do if he claims for himself a certain persona. Learning may take place through description: one is
told that men do not cry, women do not cross their legs when sitting,
and doctors do not seem uncertain of themselves when rendering a
diagnosis. One also learns roles through imitation, by watching others
play roles. No one plays all the roles he learns about, but his knowledge of others' roles allows him to synchronize his pattern of behavior with those of others. For example, a man's knowledge of the
role of wife allows him to properly perform the role of husband. A
speaker and an auditor must similarly know each other's obligations
if they are to send the appropriate verbal and nonverbal messages.

[10] Paul Ekman, Wallace Friesen, and Phoebe Ellsworth, **Emotion in the Human
Face: Guidelines for Research and a Review of Findings** (Elmsford, N.Y.:
Pergamon Press, forthcoming).

Role performance requires a great deal of effort, which is often apparent in the person who is learning a new role. The novice often attempts to act out everything he has seen or heard about a role. For example, the young doctor will consciously work at maintaining a neutral facial expression, at making gestures which are confident and sure, at appearing relaxed yet alert. These nonverbal role behaviors will, in time, become habitual.

Certain nonverbal behaviors are required of all social actors regardless of the roles which they assume. When one is in the presence of others, one must constantly signal that he is participating in the interaction by the conventionalized discourse of body idiom.

There is typically an obligation to convey certain information when in the presence of others and an obligation not to convey other impressions, just as there is an expectation that others will present themselves in certain ways.[11]

Information about involvement can be emitted by a host of nonverbal signals such as eye contact, head jerks, and appropriate facial expressions.

A performer is protected in his role by a series of social mechanisms. A number of people may join together in a team to present a unified performance, supporting one another's definition of reality. A family or a group of labor negotiators or a clique of friends can perform this function. By social and architectural arrangement, people divide their audiences. This allows for the presentation of disparate role behavior (the domineering college professor who is also a henpecked husband). Sometimes these mechanisms fail, and information damaging to self-esteem is made overt in the wrong interaction. To minimize such possibilities, people tend to avoid those who are likely to attack their self-image.

Once an individual is in the communication situation, he must maintain his identity.

He must ensure that a particular **expressive order** is sustained—an order that regulates the flow of events, large or small, so that anything that appears to be expressed by them will be consistent with his face [the idea of himself which he is projecting].[12]

[11] Erving Goffman, **Behavior in Public Places** (New York: The Free Press, 1963), pp. 34–35.
[12] Erving Goffman, **Interaction Ritual** (Garden City, N.Y.: Doubleday Anchor Books, 1967), p. 9.

Having claimed the aspect of a serious person, an individual cannot break into gales of laughter for trivial cause, nor can a person who claims competence appear to be exceedingly nervous. Indeed, discrepancies in expressive self-presentation are so disruptive that an individual who is prone to them is often thought to be mentally ill, a designation which may merely indicate that he is incapable of interacting with others in a safe way.

The duty of a person who is sustaining interaction goes beyond controlling his own behavior to include protecting others in their identities. If a person behaves badly, others have an obligation to do something to defend him. Consider a familiar case in the speech classroom: An extroverted, well-liked student rises to make his first speech. His voice cracks and he drops his notes, he repeats himself, he apologizes to the audience for his lack of preparation, and he continues with an embarrassingly bad speech, becoming visibly more disconcerted with each word. During his performance, the audience has probably grown increasingly tense. The usual **sotto voce** chatter in the back row ceases, for no one wants to distract a man who is obviously in trouble. Some auditors will turn their eyes away from the speaker, indicating that they do not want to share his discomfiture, or that the situation is too upsetting for them to endure completely. Other listeners will consciously focus on the speaker, composing a set of facial expressions which will convey to the speaker their sympathy and support. Some will squirm and others will contort their bodies much like a golfer trying to help a putted ball into the cup. After the speech is over, the audience may visibly relax, tensed bodies going limp. Some students in the class will withdraw from the situation, saying nothing. Others will claim that the speech was not bad, asserting, essentially, that what happened did not happen (here, again, conscious facial manipulation is necessary to create the appearance of sincerity). Others may claim that the speaker was not really himself, that he was asked to do the impossible, or that the speaking skill he was asked to display is a trivial way of judging his character. In each of these ways, the audience is giving the speaker a way out of the situation, allowing him to maintain his essential self-respect even though he has performed badly. Such protecting activity, of course, occurs in many different communication situations. The delayed laugh at a joke, the rapid changing of the subject when a guest touches on a taboo topic, the slight flicker of a reassuring smile when a guest accidentally drops ashes on the rug—are all verbal and nonverbal protective maneuvers.

Why do people expend so much effort to control and protect self-presentations? Let us return to what we said earlier about categorization. When we respond to others we present stylized performances. Now, which particular performance we stage at any one time depends upon the category into which we place the other interactant. Categorization is an inferential process. We observe a few behaviors, categorize the other person, and then assume that under future circumstances he will behave in ways consistent with other people in the same category. If you see a person walking down the street in sport clothes, appearing to be between the ages of 18 and 22, and carrying books under his arm, you can make the inference that he is a student, that he will speak with good grammar, that he possesses a modicum of academic knowledge, and even that he is opposed to the war in Vietnam. Should you speak to him, using long words, making reference to college affairs, and declaring your opposition to the war, your actions would be soundly based on these inferences. But suppose he then hits you with the books he is carrying since, in fact, he is a Vietnam veteran working in the construction trade who is carrying his collection of detective novels to a friend with whom he has arranged to meet at a pro-war rally. The approach which you have taken with him is not consonant with his true identity: the process of inference has gotten you into trouble.

To avoid such problems, most people remain verbally and nonverbally neutral in interacting with a stranger until his identity can be safely inferred. Even after longer acquaintance, the approach chosen must be constantly modified to accommodate suddenly revealed new characteristics. But when wholly new identities appear, the interactants are really in trouble. This may occur when a person is faking an identity, something that most people do now and again. Our problem would be in having to change the act which we have chosen. As Goffman puts it, "Should the person radically alter his line, or should it become discredited, then confusion results, for the participants will have prepared and committed themselves for actions that are now unsuitable."[13] Consequently, we need to protect other people in their identities not solely out of altruism or to demonstrate facility in social interaction, but to protect ourselves, averting the need to change our

[13] **Ibid.**, p. 12.

own behavior when new information discrediting to the other appears.

There are many ways of protecting ourselves and those with whom we interact. One way, which has a predominantly nonverbal component, is poise. Poise involves the ability not to become flustered when a situation which threatens self-esteem arises. The cultural model for poise is the upper-class Englishman or the American grande dame who reacts unemotionally to all crises. Poise has recently become known as "cool." The person who "keeps his cool" is one who, in action as well as words, does not become aroused, tense, or strongly emotive about events which seemingly undermine his credibility and that of others. At its most effective, "cool" requires the student to react passively to the news that he has just lost his after-school job, or failed to win a student body election.

Nonverbal self-presentation
and motor coordination

Self-presentation clearly requires a great deal of physical coordination between all the modalities of expression. In fact, one social psychologist persuasively describes interactive skills as primarily motor skills. Driving a car, playing tennis, riding a bicycle, and threading a needle are all motor skills which have been intensively studied by psychologists. Social interaction bears a close resemblance to these motor skills. The social actor has definite goals such as handling information, affecting another's attitudes and behaviors, and participating with others to accomplish tasks. These are goals in the same sense as maintaining one's balance while ice-skating, for in both motor skill activities and social interaction, the individual must selectively perceive certain aspects of his environment, consciously or subconsciously translate these perceptions into usable information, make exact motor responses, and rely on feedback for corrective action.[14]

Certain insights into nonverbal communication result from an attempt to compare interaction to behaviors such as riding a bicycle. The sending and receiving of nonverbal cues may become as automatic as maintaining balance. For example, the greeting ritual in America—the handshake, the smile, and the "Hello" warmly intoned—

[14] Argyle, **The Psychology of Interpersonal Behavior,** pp. 85–96.

is motoric activity practiced until it has become rote behavior. During conversation, people nod their heads and smile or frown in support or denial of what others are saying often on a completely subconscious basis. Like motor skills, interactive skills become perfected through repetitive performance. Small children have great difficulty controlling many of the behaviors which have been perfected by adults. If one wishes to learn a particular group's system of nonverbal expression, one must constantly exercise within that system. Thus, one cannot learn precisely appropriate behavior by verbal instruction, any more than a machinist can be taught skills of his trade by reading a book on the subject. Individual differences in nonverbal skills can be explained as variations in motor ability as well as by different social experiences and degree of confidence. Any two children who are given bicycles and are motivated to ride will not become equally skilled at bicycle riding because of inherent physiological differences. The same may be true of individuals whose ultimate success in using social skills depends both upon innate ability and social practice.

Like motor skills, social skills can become so well learned that they are inflexible. Each individual learns hundreds of bits of behavior, and puts the bits together in role performances. But previous learning may prevent him from improving upon the behavior which has become so habitual. An individual whose speaking gestures have become an unconscious part of his movement repertoire is generally unable to easily incorporate new, more effective movements into his communicative behavior. This drawback is partially offset because one thus need not think about many aspects of communication behavior, but can save energy for crucial activity such as the formation and expression of ideas. Training in new nonverbal skills must be presented in such a way that the learner does not become too involved in many aspects of his behavior at once. (One of the authors, who was riding a bicycle, fell off when he chanced to think about the complexity of what he was doing!)

Summary

We have seen that nonverbal expressions are signals which have informational and integrative functions. The proper performance of communicative acts is important to the psychological integrity of the individual, and such performance is, in turn, dependent upon motor abilities. However, the totality of an individual's performance cannot be judged apart from the rules which govern the particular social system of which he is a member. In the next two chapters, we will first examine how systems of nonverbal expression vary among cultures, and then take a brief look at certain aspects of nonverbal communication in the United States.

Culture and nonverbal meaning: cross-cultural studies

Nonverbal ethnocentrism

In the early 1950s, a controversy raged in American churches over the respective merits of the King James and the Revised Standard Versions of the **Bible.** Conservatives who favored the King James argued that its stately and familiar language made it superior to the Revised Standard. Modernists replied that many of the words and phrases of the King James translation were so archaic as to be indecipherable to modern readers. Before the debate had run its course, one traditionalist angrily proclaimed that she would continue to read the Gospel according to her King James: "That's the way St. Paul wrote it, and that's good enough for me." While few people today believe that St. Paul was a master of seventeenth-century English, the lady's belief that he was demonstrates a common assumption about language. Human beings tend to believe that their particular language is the universal tongue. The American tourist in Europe, trying to make himself understood by a precise pronunciation of English, is a caricature of the individual who believes that all men comprehend, or ought to comprehend, his language. Fortunately, ethnocentrism with regard to language is disappearing. Familiarity with many cultures, either through direct contact or through the mass

media and the educational process, is a common experience. Awareness that language is a fabricated tool, an arbitrary attribution of
symbolic meaning to a few of the many sound combinations which
humans can utter, can develop from even superficial intercultural
contact. Margaret Mead expressed the opinion that

> contiguity and close interrelationships between groups with differing
> communicational styles increase awareness that various aspects of the
> communicational system are learned, can be taught, and are transmis-
> sible to others who were not born to them.[1]

Apparently language ethnocentrism is fairly easily unlearned through
familiarity with other cultures. But appreciation for differences of
nonverbal communication seems to be gained more slowly.

Mere sophistication about language does not automatically lead to
decreased ethnocentrism about nonverbal communication. A nineteenth-century American explorer wrote about the Mexican population
near Taos, "I had expected to find no difference between these people
and our own, but their language. I was never so mistaken."[2] We similarly fail to recognize that differences in communication encompass
more than differences in language. The human body is capable of over
270,000 discrete gestures, a range of variations which may be greater
than the range of possible sounds. As is true with language, choosing
meaningful gestures out of a vast number of possibilities results in
wide divergence among nonverbal systems used by various cultures.
Consider the simple act of pointing. Among Europeans in both
Europe and North America, this act is rendered by pointing with the
forefinger, with the other fingers curled under the palm. American
Indians, Shans, and other Mongoloid peoples, and subsaharan Afri-
cans point with their lips. Or consider the act of attracting the attention of a waiter. In America, the customer moves his forefinger toward
himself, then away from himself, then toward himself again. A Latin
American customer would make a downward arc with his right hand
almost identical to the American jocular "away with you." The Shans
of Burma accomplish the same purpose by holding the palm down,
moving the fingers as if playing an arpeggio. Probably the waiter

---

[1] Margaret Mead, "Vicissitudes of the Study of the Total Communication Process,"
in Thomas Sebeok **et al.,** eds., **Approaches to Semiotics** (The Hague: Mouton,
1964), p. 281.
[2] James Pattie, "Personal Narrative," in R. G. Thwaites, ed., **Early Western
Travels, 1748–1846** (Cleveland: Clark, 1904–1907), XVIII, 74.

ignores the customer, regardless of the manner in which he gestures (see Figure 6–1).

Just as words carry denotative and connotative meanings, gestures have emotional overtones as well as designative significance. Waiters in India are summoned by a click of the fingers which, on the face of it, is an inconspicuous and efficient gesture. But such a gesture might elicit anger from an American waiter. For us, snapping fingers for service is the act of a superior asserting power over a menial. As such, finger snapping as a call for service is a violation of the democratic ethos. To take a more extreme case, Indian women show deference to their superiors by uncovering the upper half of their bodies. This act would be interpreted in the West as a sign of neurotic or psychotic exhibitionism, or of a knowledge about the latest in **haute couture.**

Figure 6–1. Different hand signals for calling a waiter

Comparison of nonverbal systems

Cross-cultural differences in nonverbal communications are not limited to stylized gestures, but include many meaningful movements that seem autonomic. Birdwhistell asserts that,

> Kutenai Indians could tell the difference between a Kutenai cough and a Shuswap cough. . . . The Kutenai Indians coughed up their nose. This is part of being a decent Kutenai and not to have done so would mean being taken for a damned Shuswap![3]

Moreover, the observation of differences has gone beyond the folklorists' mania for collecting peculiarities. Serious work is now being

[3] Ray Birdwhistell, "Discussion Session on Psychiatry," in Thomas Sebeok **et al.,** eds., **Approaches to Semiotics** (The Hague: Mouton, 1964), p. 42.

done to delineate the role played by culture at all levels of the communication process. Although we still consider the biological and psychological forces discussed in the preceding chapter to be important, the significance of an individual's behavior "can only be assessed following the analysis of the larger system of which his is a part."[4] Many years ago, the distinguished anthropologist Franz Boas articulated a relationship which we should now examine. He wrote: "the behavior of the individual depends upon his own anatomical and physiological make-up, over which is superimposed the important influence of social and geographic environment in which he lives."[5] By comparing nonverbal systems across a variety of cultures, we can gain a better idea of the ways culture influences communication.

Comparison of postural communication

Anthropologists study culture in two different ways. They can choose to describe a culture exhaustively, or they may compare one aspect of a culture with comparable aspects of another. The first approach is exemplified by a field study of a remote African tribe, the second by efforts to compare child-rearing practices in several cultures. Using field studies as his source of information, Gordon Hewes has made a preliminary effort at describing differences between the basic postures of various societies.[6] He admits that certain postures are universal, such as the upright stance with the arms hanging down at the sides. However, postures which we often regard as universal are peculiar to our own culture. Hewes reports that in Japan, individuals sometimes squat on their heels in theater seats. This behavior is not a matter of "not knowing better," but a matter of feeling more comfortable. Japanese are accustomed to sitting on the floor. Like nearly one-quarter of the world's population, they feel more natural in this position than in the chair-sitting posture. As with gestures, many postural alternatives are open to man. There are about 1,000 different steady postures which a human body can assume. Consequently, it is not surprising to find a range of sitting postures extending from

[4] Alfred S. Hayes, "Paralinguistics and Kinesics: Pedagogical Perspectives," in Thomas Sebeok **et al.,** eds., **Approaches to Semiotics** (The Hague: Mouton, 1964), p. 159.
[5] Franz Boas, "Foreword," in David Efron, **Gesture and Environment** (New York: King's Crown Press, 1941), p. x.
[6] Gordon Hewes, "The Anthropology of Posture," **Scientific American,** CLXLVI (1957), 123–32.

chair-sitting to squatting to sitting cross-legged. Nor is it surprising to find representative individuals folding their arms across their chests, or resting both arms by clasping the hands around the back of the neck.

Figure 6–2. Cultural variation in resting positions

We do not know with much certainty why some cultures choose certain postures and ignore other possibilities. Hewes writes that "a whole complex of factors—anatomical, physiological, cultural, environmental, technological—is involved in the evolution of the many different postural habits that the peoples of the earth have assumed." Structural variance among races might provide a clue to variance of posture. From a purely biomechanical point of view, long-legged groups might display a different posture than short-legged people. However, a persuasive case has not been made proving that differences among cultural groups can best be explained by genetic differences, for various cultures of a single race show wide postural variance. And intraculturally, individuals with greatly different physiological profiles show greater similarity of posture than like individuals of different cultures. Learning seems to be a more important factor than race or idiosyncratic physical differences in creating postural variation (see Figure 6–2).

Environmental factors may also shape posture. A person does not normally sit on the ground if it is cold and wet. Similarly, a herdsman in a high-grass area would stand as he watched his flock, although he could do the same job in short grass while squatting or sitting. Technology modifies the environment, and may have a direct effect upon postural behavior—for example, a textile factory with a machine which causes the operator to constantly stoop. Moreover, architecture can be conducive to certain postures: "houses built on platforms or with porches, affording the opportunity for dangling the legs over the edge, help develop sitting habits which call for furniture."[7] This should not lead to the conclusion, however, that men sit in chairs because chairs were invented. The invention of the chair is not as important as its widespread adoption, and the decision to use an available type of furniture depends upon culture. Societies often refrain from doing many things which are technologically feasible because of opposing traditional preferences.

Comparison of movement communication

The ways human beings move are as various as the manner in which they sit or stand. In fact, posture influences movement style. Alan Lomax and his colleagues elaborate the concept of posture into that of "body attitude," the position "from which the individuals in a culture develop their activities and from which their movement unfolds." Lomax argues that "in simple cultures most individuals tend to adopt the same body attitude no matter what the activity and in spite of differences of age and sex." The adoption of a generalized body attitude serves two purposes: it distinguishes members from non-

[7] Ibid.

members, instantly indicating who has been trained in the group's movement patterns, and it molds the movement of the entire group in many different activities, providing "key patterns in all sorts of behavior within one culture." Using this concept, Lomax narrowed the scope of his investigation, asserting that dance, the most formalized pattern of movement, reflects the more general patterning of everyday life.[8]

Lomax used his choreographic approach to discover numerous differences between the movement patterns of cultures. On the most general level, he noticed that some cultures employ one-unit body movements, as if the trunk were a solid, block-like structure. The waltz is based on a one-unit system. Other cultures use a two-unit system, moving the upper and lower trunk separately. Belly dancing is based on the two-unit system. Describing body movement another way, he found that some cultures engage in only a few basic movements. Aboriginal dancers in Australia "generally move the whole leg or arm rather than using these limbs segmentally." At the other end of the scale, Indian dancers use many more body parts, including eyebrow, eye, mouth, and finger movement as integral parts of their performance. Between these two extremes lies a gradient of increasing complexity.

In explaining differences such as these, Lomax asserts that a correlation exists between economic activity and type of movement system. He writes that "primitive people employ a smaller number of body parts in any given moment in dance and everyday life than do people of complex cultures." For example, when the plow is introduced into a primitive agricultural society, the farmers' complexity of movement increases, and rises sharply once again with the advent of irrigation techniques—a further improvement. This connection between economic life and movement is even more clear in the distinction between one- and two-unit body movements. The trunk when used as one unit is effective for up-and-down and back-and-forth movements, which are important in hunting and fishing. The two-unit system, which involves twisting at the waist, is well adapted to the activities of African millet agriculture: seeding, hoeing, and harvesting. Lomax also relates the two-unit system to the erotic orientation of African and Oceanic cultures: "The independently rotating pelvis, so clear

[8] Alan Lomax, **Folk Song Style and Culture** (Washington, D.C.: American Association for the Advancement of Science, 1968), pp. 235–47.

in African behavior and dance . . . mimes, recalls, and reinforces the sexual act, especially the woman's part in it." The erotic orientation, in turn, is explained as necessary for maintaining the central institutions of African society—polygamy and rapidly expanding villages based on lineage.

This analysis of movement styles illustrates both the uses and the hazards of cultural comparisons. By defining the components of movement, Lomax provides a tool for comparing cultures on an unexplored level, a tool which anthropologists can use to test the hypothesis that the same body attitudes and movements occur in many contexts within a single culture. Dominant movement styles, once defined, could become a rather precise index for measuring the similarity of human groups. And when they are linked with other kinds of studies, measurements of movements can tell us a great deal about cultural evolution. Moreover, communication specialists might well wish to determine whether similarities of movement correlate with similarities in other types of verbal and nonverbal behavior.

However, Lomax moves beyond methods of comparison to an assertion of causation, where he unfortunately runs afoul of one of the hazards of cross-cultural research. He labels the two-unit movements of African and Polynesian dancers erotic, but the present authors must protest that what may appear to western eyes to be erotic may not be at all erotic to the performers. Any meanings which we attach to certain gestures and movements cannot be regarded as universal without proof. Researchers cannot judge behavior in other cultures by assuming that the performers must feel as Americans feel about that behavior. The relation between movement and psychic life needs exploration, and no amount of speculation can make up for the present paucity of such investigation.

Lomax also argues that the type of economic activity, at least in simple societies, influences movement repertoires, such that movement becomes more elaborate as agricultural methods are improved. But one cannot so easily step from correlation to causation. An equally likely explanation is that other factors such as contact with another culture simultaneously cause changes in both technology and movement patterns. In even the simplest culture, the overwhelming complexity of human motivation defies facile attempts to explain the origin of differences.

Nor can information be generalized from simple tradition-bound societies to more complex ones. In both western Europe and the United States in recent years, the dominant mode of dancing has changed from a one-unit to a two-unit system. This change cannot easily be attributed to changing patterns of economic activities or to the need for an increased birth rate. Partially valid social and psychological explanations have been offered, many of which have little relevance for simpler societies. Changing styles, which are connected with a phenomenon called the "youth revolution," may result from the influence of our black subculture, may be a rejection of previous esthetic forms, or may simply be an adoption of a generally "looser" life style. Changes in movement patterns in primitive and advanced societies may eventually prove to be fertile ground for comparative research. Thus, we might be badly mistaken to make premature attempts at generalization.

There is little doubt that kinesic activity is, to a large degree, culture-bound. Many of the better foreign movies imported into the United States are dubbed into English by the use of a process called "lip-synching." The lip-syncher, provided with a rough translation of the script, slowly runs a print of the film through a movieola, attempting to find English equivalents which fit the lip movements of the actors. The synched script is then read by actors and dubbed in. Despite the high quality of much of this work, watching a lip-synched movie can still be an amusing experience, for although the words fit the lips, they don't fit facial expressions, movements, or posture. French actors seem to say things in English which require certain sweeping gestures. But the "right" movements are missing, for the actors are still gesturing in the tighter, more exact French manner.

While he was visiting a French mental hospital, Birdwhistell observed what was to him a disconcerting experience—a mental patient who said only a few quiet words and who was engaged in broad and aggressive gestures. Such gestures, said Birdwhistell, were far different from those he had come to expect from French speakers. Whereas in dubbed movies the words had been wrong and the gestures right, Birdwhistell heard the right words emerge from a patient whose body activity was wrong.[9] Nonverbal languages, then, seem to be as indicative of membership in a certain cultural group, and as different from one another, as verbal languages.

[9] Ray Birdwhistell, "Discussion Session on Language Teaching," in Thomas Sebeok **et al.**, eds., **Approaches to Semiotics** (The Hague: Mouton, 1964), p. 179.

Another method for comparing cultures is based on Birdwhistell's notational system which we described in Chapter 2. We can facilitate the comparison of cultures by attempting to reduce posture, movement, and facial expressions to exact descriptions. Since this system is based on a linguistic model, its use raises the possibility of developing a kinesic grammar for every culture, just as grammars have been developed for languages.

The multilingual individual provides a study in the relation of verbal and nonverbal languages. Mayor Fiorello La Guardia of New York was able to speak most effectively to his constituents in Italian and Yiddish, as well as in English. If La Guardia were alive today and were to speak on television, a person who is familiar with the kinesic profiles of individuals from the cultures in which these three languages are spoken would be able to turn off the sound and still identify the language La Guardia would be speaking. Individuals who are in the process of learning a second language, however, have difficulty coordinating their new verbal expressions with their old nonverbal expressions. The problem is exacerbated by current teaching methods. Students are required by hoary tradition to sit motionless in a language laboratory or classroom, learning to make proper sounds, giving no thought whatsoever to proper movement. A fixed conception of classroom decorum and the absence of nonverbal models may inhibit second-language learning, and they certainly prevent students from learning a second communication system. Moreover, if we fail to recognize that non-English speakers often learn our language in the same stilted way we learn theirs, we can easily get our signals mixed. Second-language learners who have only begun to learn a new set of movements may well make kinesic mistakes, or slip back into their original mode of expression. Consequently, we may mistake expressions of friendliness for gestures of hostility, or signs of irritation for indications of interest. For example, one of the most repeated maxims in the study of public address is that speakers must maintain "eye-contact" with members of their audience. Failure to maintain this visual directness for us is a sign of stage fright or insincerity. But in many cultures, an unstated rule forbids eye contact. One anthropologist reports that certain groups of Indians do not

> look at the person addressed any more than the latter watches the speaker. Both look at some outside objects. This is also the attitude of

the Indian when addressing more than one listener, so that he appears to be talking to someone not visibly present.[10]

Therefore, as we have seen, individuals who act within a system other than the one which we know can easily violate our most cherished unstated rules.

Once certain postures and movements become habitual in a society, they are invested with esthetic and moral significance. Though we rarely think about it, we form judgments about proper ways to sit, stand, and move. Rudolf Laban describes and attempts to explain this phenomenon:

> Any deviation from the main fashion or style of an epoch has been looked upon as abnormal. . . . That such deviations have even been considered ugly and wrong is due to a peculiarity of the human herd instinct. Communities seem to regard a certain uniformity of movement behavior as indispensable for safeguarding the stability of the community spirit.[11]

Despite the continuing demonstration by anthropologists that no single set of motor habits is inherently superior to any other, we continue to apply the arbitrary standards which we have learned to individuals who have been trained in other cultures. As part of the socialization process, children in America learn that it is effeminate for men to dramatize their emotions, or provocative for women to move their hips too much when they walk. By these standards, Latin men are effeminate and Latin women sensual. At the same time, we deride other groups for an excess of the American virtue of stoicism. The Chinese, who mask their facial reactions more than we do, are said to be inscrutable.

Comparison of proxemic communication

The most widely known scholar of comparative nonverbal communication is Edward Hall, whose research in proxemics, the study of man's use of space, has already been mentioned. He has dealt with spacing between communicators, that behavior which has been most thoroughly investigated by students of proxemics. Hall notes that in

[10] T. Whiffen, **The Northwest Amazons** (London: Constable, 1915), p. 254.
[11] Rudolf Laban, **The Mastery of Movement on the Stage** (London: McDonald and Evans, 1950), p. 94.

American culture, individuals establish different distances between themselves and the people with whom they are conversing. On the basis of such a relationship between the nature of a communication situation and the distance between sender and receiver, Hall delineates four general distance categories, each with a close and a far phase. The first category is "intimate distance." In its close phase, this is the distance of "love-making and wrestling, comforting and protecting." Individuals who are from six to eighteen inches apart are in the far phase of intimate distance. In American middle-class culture, this proxemic relationship is used for private contact between individuals who are emotionally involved with one another. Informal contact between friends is usually carried on at "personal distance," between one and one half and four feet. Acquaintances usually communicate at a range of four to twelve feet, which Hall calls "social distance." Close colleagues tend to communicate in the close phase of social distance, whereas people meeting in an office for the first time tend to assume the far phase. At approximately twelve feet, communicators enter the "public distance" range of highly formalized social contact. At the far phase of public distance, communication becomes stylized into public speaking.

If the nature of the communication situation—the people involved and the purpose of talking—influences distal relationships, then those relationships influence other verbal and nonverbal expressions. For example, linguists have observed that a speaker at public distance carefully chooses his words and phrasing of sentences, as well as his grammar and syntax. That is, at a point about twelve feet from the auditor, a speaker becomes formal. At an intimate distance, people usually whisper, and they only speak in normal tones at the far phase of personal distance. Nonverbal communication at intimate distance involves many senses—touch, heat, smell, and minute gestures. But at public distances, most of the body's sense receptors are no longer operable, and much nonverbal communication consists of exaggerated gestures and shifts of body stance. The relationship between proxemics and other modes of communication well illustrates the close integration of the many different methods of transmitting meaning.

The distances just described have been observed in middle-class Americans, but they are not universal. Arabs, for example, have an entirely different attitude toward spatial relationships in public places. Whereas an individual's right to occupy a particular space is usually respected in America, the Arab has a different notion. For the latter, public literally means public, and the fact that someone occupies space in a line, on a streetcorner, or in a theater seat means precious little. If the Arab wants a space, he thinks nothing of standing indecently close (by American standards) until the occupant of that space literally gives it up in disgust:

> In Beirut only the hardy sit in the last row in a movie theatre, because there are usually standees who want seats and who push and shove and make such a nuisance that most people give up and leave.[12]

However, whereas proxemic relationships, like other forms of communication, are arbitrary, we invest them with emotional significance. We may become uneasy and uncertain when the wrong person communicates the wrong message at the wrong distance. Consequently, an American's equanimity is upset when an Arab acquaintance invades the intimate distance to speak an impersonal message. And the Arab feels abused because the American insists on moving away from him, outside the zone which the Arab defines as proper for polite conversation.

What causes cultures to define differently the proper distances of communication? Hall argues that cultures establish preferences in the use of sense modalities. General ranges of distance are established by the main senses of sight and hearing, but some cultures extensively employ smell and touch, whereas others make no use of them, implicitly forbidding communication in these modes. Arabs often converse closely enough to smell one another's breath and body odor. They employ subtle differences in odor to learn something about the emotions and personality of even casual acquaintances. In the United States, only the refreshing smell of a lively mouthwash is acceptable, and then only among intimates. Similarly, with regard to touch, Americans are largely a "hands off" culture in which physical contact is a clear sign of intimacy, except in certain stylized expressions of friendship. For Arabs, however, touching colleagues or even strangers in the street is perfectly permissible. Casual messages can often be transmitted in this way.

Attributing proxemic variations between cultures to learned sense

[12] Edward Hall, **Hidden Dimension** (Garden City, N.Y.: Doubleday & Company, Inc., 1966), pp. 116–25, 156.

preferences is only part of the explanation of variations in distance patterning. What causes sense preferences to vary? Hall feels that in part, cultures impress different visions of self on their members. In northern Europe and America, one thinks of himself as coterminous with his skin, and possibly with his clothes and with a small area of space around him. But Arabs do not share this conception. They locate the "self," Hall asserts, deep within the body. Consequently, the skin is perceived as somewhat unrelated to self, as are body odors. Impersonal touching and smelling, then, are perfectly permissible, for a stranger is not really touching the self. Extending the argument further, one has to ask whether the sense of self is learned. There is a great deal of well-supported theory which suggests that this basic perception is indeed the result of early childhood training, and is therefore malleable by culture. One sociologist has summarized this point of view by writing that, "the self is established, maintained, and altered in and through communication."[13]

Culture, personality, and expression

At least one study confirms a relationship among early childhood training, the sense of self, and expressive behavior.[14] The investigators hypothesized that members of different cultures would vary in the definiteness of body image boundary. A review of Rorschach protocols administered in a variety of cultures revealed that some groups had a definite image of their body boundary (Bhils, Navahos, and Zuñis) and that other groups manifested an indefinite boundary sense (Haitians, Americans). The former, the definite boundary groups, are very permissive in their early child-raising practices, allowing children to order freely their way of life and express their feelings. These groups also train a child to accept a definite and unambiguous code of values. The low-boundary groups, however, show a tendency to subscribe to highly rigid child-raising practices and to indoctrinate children into a complex and often contradictory value system. In general, the effect of these two systems on communicative behavior is to encourage greater openness of expression for the high-boundary groups and greater masking of emotion for the low-boundary groups.

[13] Gregory P. Stone, "Appearance and the Self," in Arnold Rose, ed., **Human Behavior and Social Processes** (Boston: Houghton Mifflin, 1962), p. 86.
[14] Seymour Fisher, **Body Image and Personality** (New York: Van Nostrand Rinehold, 1958), pp. 277–97.

And although these results are, at best, tentative, they support the possibility that nonverbal communication does not merely cause the child to imitate the behavior of his elders, or make a capricious choice among many possible alternative behaviors. Such differences in behavior may be deeply embedded within the world-view and assumptions which are an inherent part of each culture.

Ethnicity and tolerance

There is, of course, a moral in Hall's study of proxemics. Just as most works in cultural anthropology have implicitly taught understanding and tolerance for alien cultures, so Hall reminds us that failure to properly read the nonverbal messages sent to us by members of other cultures can lead to tension and conflict. And although misunderstanding is extremely dangerous in international relations, it is most pervasive in the United States with its highly heterogeneous population. As Nathan Glazer and Daniel Moynihan demonstrate, ethnic groups beyond the second generation have retained many of the traits which their forebears brought with them from other cultures. They believe, however, that immigrants soon lose their distinct language and culture.[15] There is debate on the extent to which nonverbal systems of communication are retained by the sons and daughters of immigrants. Hall argues that ethnic groups tend to retain their key assumptions about nonverbal communication: "Superficially, these groups may all look alike and sound somewhat alike but beneath the surface there lie manifold unstated, unformulated differences in the structuring of time, space, materials, and relationships."[16] A number of studies of ethnic enclaves, most notably the study by Herbert Gans, argue that distinct ways of establishing and maintaining human relations continue through generations.[17] These arguments are counterbalanced, however, by several field studies which found that the more obvious differences in communicative behavior tend to disappear. David Efron, working in the early 1940s, found that ethnic differences were very marked among first-generation immigrants: "The radius of the gestures of the ghetto Jew seems to be much more confined than

[15] Nathan Glazer and Daniel Moynihan, **Beyond the Melting Pot** (Cambridge, Mass.: The M.I.T. Press, 1963), pp. v–vi, 13.
[16] Hall, **Hidden Dimension,** p. x.
[17] Herbert Gans, **The Urban Villagers** (New York: The Free Press, 1962), pp. 20–21, 33, 35.

that of the Southern Italian." In later generations, these differences disappear.[18] Several recent field studies have found little difference in proxemic behavior among different ethnic groups.[19] Although further research must be done to determine degrees of difference in non-verbal behavior among individuals with different cultural back-grounds, a great deal of impressionistic evidence supports the notion that ethnic tensions are attributable in some degree to misunder-standings of nonverbal messages.

In black and white relations, for example, there is a tendency to misunderstand communication by touch. As one writer points out,

> The white man is bewildered by the hand on the shoulder, the clap on the back, the slap on the palm, so characteristic of the excitement of communication among black people. The black is dismayed by the "coldness" of his white respondent. Mistrust is the result.[20]

And this mistrust may be engendered in the classroom when the teacher and students are of different races.

We are not suggesting here that nonverbal misunderstandings are more important or even equally as important as a host of other sources of ethnic conflict. But differences in methods of communication do create tensions which make comfortable interchange of ideas less possible. There is some truth to the notion that we are a country integrated between 9 and 5, and that after work we all seek people with whom we can communicate, who are culturally attuned to our signals. If we continue this condition because we have failed to reach across cultural boundaries, everyone is robbed of personal enrichment and the nation is bereft of social tranquility.

Summary

The best way to discover the role of culture in shaping nonverbal communication is to examine the differences and similarities in

[18] David Efron, **Gesture and Environment** (New York: King's Crown Press, 1941), pp. 43, 136.
[19] Robert Forsten, and Charles Larson, "The Dynamics of Space," **Journal of Communication**, XVIII (1968), 109–16; Stanley Jones, "Nonverbal Communication in the Streets: A Comparative Analysis of Dyadic Interaction in Selected Sub-Cultures of New York City," unpublished paper presented at the Annual Convention of the Speech Association of America, New York, 1969.
[20] Gerald Phillips **et al., The Development of Oral Communication in the Classroom** (Indianapolis: The Bobbs-Merrill Company, Inc., 1970), pp. 171, 184.

expressive behavior between cultures. In this chapter, we have emphasized those differences, and we have found great variety in the forms of nonverbal expression in various societies. This variety is not a matter of caprice or random choice, for the communicative behavior of any culture springs from the tacit assumptions and mental habits of its members.

SEVEN

Culture and nonverbal meaning: a study in American behavioral patterns

At the end of the last chapter, we noted that many different subcultures exist in the United States, each of which has a set of nonverbal meanings which it does not share with the others. The case for the extreme diversity of nonverbal systems can be put even more strongly. Every group of people develops specific signals which have little meaning to outsiders. For example, a class may learn that the professor is bored when he jingles the change in his pocket, and although change-jingling is not a signal with invariant meaning within the academic community or a particular college, it is extremely expressive in communication between this particular professor and his students. This kind of nonverbal meaning, evolved within small groups, can only be learned by actual observation of communication situations. However, we can make some observations here, which are valid for most groups in the United States, about a variety of nonverbal **cues.** For convenience, we have grouped these cues under the headings of eye movement, facial expression, body movement, spatial relationships, and personal appearance and clothing.

Eye movement

Eye movement serves several social purposes. First, by looking at people's eyes, individuals gather much nonverbal information about other people. Second, looking at another person indicates that the channels of communication are open. In fact, one of the requirements for full social engagement is that the participants look at one another. When a person says, "Pay attention to what I am saying," he usually means, "Look at me." However, the direction of gaze may modify the message sent by facial expression. For example, when a person's face indicates he is angry, the direction of his gaze may indicate the object of his anger. Third, being looked at is a potent stimulus.[1] For example, speakers sometimes change their strategy to deal with an audience which does not look at them, and many individuals will evade the eyes of another whose gaze is disconcertingly constant and direct.

Much research has been done on eye contact, or mutual gaze interaction. Eye contact is established when two people look at one another's eyes. For a speaker, eye contact occurs at the end of phrases and sentences, when he glances up from his text, and it ceases to occur during long statements.[2] When two people like one another, they establish eye contact more often and for longer duration than when there is tension in the relationship.[3]

By the use of these and other findings, several social psychologists have developed theories about relationships among personality, situation, and eye contact. Ralph Exline hypothesizes that a connection exists between visual interaction and desires for domination or warm human contact. Those who prefer "communion over control" look significantly more at others while they are speaking, except in competitive situations, when high affiliators tend to engage in less mutual glancing, and low affiliators tend to increase such activity. Interestingly, this reversing effect is considerably stronger among women than among men. Exline proposes two explanations: First, in a competitive setting task-oriented, low-affiliative individuals glance more at one another because, "in a rivalrous situation the intimacy inherent in the mutual glance would be perceived as the intimacy of combat, an intimacy more repellent to the communion-oriented person than his control-oriented counterpart." Second, women are more affected

[1] James Gibson and Anne Pick, "Perception of Another Person's Looking Behavior," **American Journal of Psychology,** LXXXVI (1963), 386–94.
[2] Ralph Exline, David Gray, and Dorothy Schuette, "Visual Behavior in a Dyad as Affected by Interview Content and Sex of Respondent," **Journal of Personality and Social Psychology,** I (1965), 201–9.
[3] These findings are summarized in Michael Argyle and Janet Dean, "Eye-Contact, Distance and Affiliation," **Sociometry,** XXVIII (1965), 289–304.

by certain task variables than men because they rely more heavily on visual cues. Exline asserts that women "may look at other persons more than do men because they value more highly the kinds of information they can obtain through such activity." This would explain why women establish more visual interaction than men in noncompetitive situations and less visual interaction than men in competitive ones. In the former case, women are using gaze to establish communion; in the latter, women are trying to reduce the unpleasant visual stimuli of others' facial cues indicating the rejection and antagonism generated by competition. These explanations are speculative, but it is nevertheless clear that a relationship exists among situational and personality variables, sex, and eye contact.[4]

Eye contact is also related to the expression of intimacy. Suppose that the primary components of intimacy are eye contact, physical proximity, intimacy of topic, and the frequency of smiling. Suppose also that people move toward an equilibrium of intimacy by establishing satisfactory relationships for each of these components. If a person moves closer to you and the situation becomes too intimate, you can restore equilibrium by moving further away, by reducing eye contact, by changing to a less intimate topic, or by smiling less often. If none of these things can be done, both you and your conversational partner will become uncomfortable, for if the situation is too intimate, you will fear rejection or the disclosure of information which should best be hidden (see Figure 7–1). If the situation is not intimate enough, however, you will feel a lack of emotional content in the interaction. Just where the equilibrium is established depends upon a host of factors. In experimental, fairly well-controlled situations, Exline has found that at least one of the behaviors predicted by the intimacy hypothesis occurs: when the discussion topic is less intimate, there is more eye contact. Argyle and Dean have conducted further experiments which show that greater proximity results in less eye contact, and that this effect is more marked for opposite- than for same-sex pairs. Moreover, they have shown that an individual will stand much closer to another person whose eyes are closed—that is, if eye contact is reduced to zero. In summary of their findings, Argyle and Dean

[4] Ralph Exline, "Explorations in the Process of Person Perception: Visual Interaction in Relation to Competition, Sex, and Need for Affiliation," **Journal of Personality,** XXXI (1963), 1–20.

*Figure 7–1. The relationship between
eye contact, distance, and intimacy*

write that "reducing eye-contact makes greater proximity possible and that greater proximity reduces eye-contact."[5] This set of findings dramatically illustrates the close relationship between the various kinds of nonverbal signalling systems operative in a social interaction.

Facial expression

Earlier we discussed research on facial expression in connection with the question of whether interpretation of faces is an innate or a socially learned behavior. Most of the experiments generated by this issue involved the showing of photographs of subjects' faces in isolation, unconnected with images of their bodies or with eliciting circumstances. In interpersonal communication, of course, faces are not

[5] Argyle and Dean, "Eye-Contact, Distance and Affiliation," p. 304.

perceived in isolation. What, then, is the relationship of facial expression to the total communication situation and to other orders of nonverbal communication?

In the 1950s, researchers who generally thought faces convey little expressive meaning argued that the context of a situation allows observers to construe the meaning of facial expressions. If the observers saw an eliciting circumstance which would normally cause pain, they described the facial expression caused by the circumstance as showing pain. Thus, context rather than actual facial expression seemed to convey meaning. Recent analysis of the experimental literature, however, redresses the balance in favor of the facial expression. Ekman and his associates argue that neither the face nor the context can carry the burden of expressive meaning. If the meaning of a facial expression is clear, and the context in which it occurs is ambiguous, then the face is the most salient message source. If the reverse is true, then the context will carry the most meaning.

The notion of both face and context as message sources is compounded from three factors: ambiguity, message complexity, and strength. A message is ambiguous if observers cannot agree on its meaning, complex if a single source relays more than one meaning at a time, and strong in relation to the intensity of emotion expressed. The first of these criteria is fairly simple. If 30 observers render 10 different judgments on one facial expression, then the face is ambiguous. The problem is more elusive if the face expresses several messages simultaneously. For example, the upper part of the face may express anger, while the mouth area indicates grief. This blend allows for a greater variety of interpretation, and a consequent confusion over meaning. The intensity of a facial message can also vary, with one face indicating great sorrow, another mild relief. The former would probably convey clearer meaning than the latter. Context can also vary along these dimensions, leading to conflicting judgments about the context, the several possible messages suggested by it, and the degree of intensity involved.[6]

The relationship between face and context has not been definitively studied with regard to source clarity. Still, the idea provides a tool for understanding an important aspect of nonverbal communication: Dif-

6 Paul Ekman, Wallace Friesen, and Phoebe Ellsworth, **Emotion in the Human Face: Guidelines for Research and a Review of Findings** (Elmsford, N.Y.: Pergamon Press, forthcoming).

ferent individuals convey an amount of information through different nonverbal channels according to the clarity with which they use each channel. For example, most students in speech classes are admonished to speak clearly and to express their ideas in unambiguous language. But who is told to make his facial expression clear? To be sure, some teachers work to suppress their students' ungainly mannerisms, but this is only the equivalent of correcting habitual mispronunciations of certain words, and probably no more effective. Certainly, however, one element of an effective communicative style is a modicum of conscious control over facial expression in order to transmit meaning decisively. But such control ought to be extended to the other levels of nonverbal expression as well.

A word of caution is in order about expressive clarity. One ought not to attempt to be clear nonverbally on all channels. To extend the analogy already begun, one can shout with his face as well as with his voice. An overly expressive face can drown out other levels of meaning, and so can hyperactive gesticulation. Some speakers defeat their purpose by attracting visual and not aural attention. This danger should not, however, prevent you from considering what mix of messages to send with greater or lesser clarity.

Most Americans are not likely to be too expressive in their facial behavior. Our social rules generally require the masking of certain emotional reactions, and this seems to be true in all other cultures as well. In America, the fashion runs to stoicism, an avoidance of exaggerated expressive behavior. An extremely angry man is required to present a neutral public face, whereas an unhappy person is allowed only barest hint of downturned lips. In other cultures excessive emotional display acts as a mask. For example, indifference to the death of a distant relative is masked by copious tears and the gnashing of teeth. The extent to which facial expression is masked is a function of both the culture and the communication situation. Among strangers, neutrality of expression is the rule. Who smiles on the subway? Conversely, the person who does not at least pretend to lower his guard among intimates by engaging in extensive facial expression is in danger of being judged cold or aloof. Ultimately, masking allows for the effective coordination of communication styles. General cultural rules about how and when to emote provide rough guidelines for the meshing of the social skills which are necessary for the establishment of good interpersonal relationships.

Posture

Postural set communicates meaning, is learned, and is significant in social interaction. James, on the basis of a series of judgment studies in which he used a variously arranged human mannequin as a stimulus, concludes that "postures do give clues to attitude, and that placement of the trunk and head contributes most to the interpretations of posture."[7] Posture is to an extent a socialized behavior. In addition to certain genetic characteristics which influence postural set, we learn to hold our bodies in certain ways by emulating primary and peer group models. The socialized nature of posture was underscored in the previous chapter where we presented data to show wide variance in body carriage from culture to culture.

Posture is a mode of expression in social exchange. Body carriage expresses both the feelings and the role of the player. A stooped college professor is playing a traditional role, but a round-backed soldier is not. Some roles require an individual to express pride and self-confidence through posture, as in the case of the general with the ram-rod spine. Other role descriptions implicitly demand an appearance of submissiveness, expressed by the waiter with stooped shoulders and slightly bowed head.

There is a wide latitude within roles for the expression of feelings relevant to a situation. A student can be interested or disinterested in a class, and his posture will reflect his degree of involvement. He will tend to lean into the center of a group if he is interested in what is happening, and he will lean away if he is not. This sort of cue transcends the role of student, of course, and is a generalized body idiom used by individuals playing many roles. In similar fashion, posture indicates the degree of social tension, as in a heated exchange when the interactants are likely to sit or stand more erect than usual.

Posture indicates when a person is changing roles, or when he is going out of—or ignoring—role. Moments before he is ready to speak, a student may sit up straight, then walk stiffly to the podium, stand erect, walk with Prussian precision back to his seat, and resume his usual slouch. He has gone through two changes, from student as bored listener to student as speaker, and then back again to bored

---

[7] W. James, "A Study of the Expression of Bodily Posture," **Journal of General Psychology**, VII (1932), 405–36.

listener. The same sorts of postural transformations occur in small group discussions in which a person may have two quite definite postural sets, one for speaking and another for listening. People can also go out of role, as when during a dull meeting some members may discard all pretense of playing their assigned parts and drop into an extremely relaxed posture (see Figure 7–2).

Figure 7–2

Movement as gesture

The line between posture and gesture cannot be clearly drawn. The very concept "gesture" seems to be of little use in the study of nonverbal communication, but it will probably continue to serve as a sort of shorthand for some very specific body movements. Usually, a gesture is thought of as a movement of hands and arms, but the whole body is capable of a single gesture, as when a person quickly leans back in his chair to indicate surprise or disagreement. Is the lifting of an eyebrow a gesture? Probably, if a gesture is defined as a visible body movement which carries expressive meaning. Here, however, we shall work from a more common definition, essentially circumscribing the concept of gesture to movements of the extremities.

Gestures can dramatically convey meaning. Apart from elaborated codes of sign language, gestures can communicate affective states. Carmichael and his colleagues studied judgments of emotions using hands as the stimulus. An actor arranged his hands to portray certain emotions; when subjects were later shown photographs of these manual gestures, they were substantially in agreement as to the emotions conveyed. The emotions most consistently judged were pleading, thoughtfulness, surprise, and fear. In a second experiment, determination, anxiety, warning, and satisfaction were best judged.[8] Reports such as these do not tell us much about the relation of hand movements and other gestures to different types of nonverbal cues or to the communication contexts in which they occur, nor do they separate culture-specific expressions from pan-cultural expressions. Although we feel that this sort of research should be extended, we can make only a minimal generalization at the present time: hand movements convey meaning which enters the stream of interaction.

One basic difference between the ways in which individuals present themselves nonverbally is in the use of gestures: some people gesture broadly and some narrowly, some often and some seldom. The same is true for other kinds of nonverbal cues. Individuals vary in the use of facial movement, paralinguistic devices, and so on for all types of nonverbal signals. However, frequency and style of gesture seem to be extremely salient to observers, especially in public speaking situations. To attain the proper degree of gesticulation, some speech teachers impose a stylized form of gesture on their students, which unfortunately misses, or at least ignores, the connection between gesture and effective communication. If effective interaction occurs when communication styles mesh—the notion we developed in Chapter 4—then movement must not be routinized but diversified to fit a variety of social situations and persons. Mechanical training in gesticulation is meant for formal speaking situations; it is not appropriate in learning to relate to others in less structured environments.

Gestures and other body movements must mesh on a level other than frequency and style, a level that might be designated **myokinetic rhythm.** People move at different rates, those who move more slowly

[8] L. Carmichael, S. Roberts, and N. Wessell, "A Study of the Judgment of Manual Expressions as Presented in Still and Motion Pictures," **Journal of Social Psychology,** VIII (1937), 115–42.

being **hypokinetic,** those who move more rapidly being **hyperkinetic.** Generally, hyperkinetic and hypokinetic people can easily annoy one another. It is exasperating for one who moves rapidly to be placed in a communication situation in which the other person responds slowly. Myokinetic variations may be caused, particularly in extreme cases, by physiology, and in other instances by cultural patterning or role prescriptions. Clearly, there are differences between cultural groups and between people in different roles as to what is considered an appropriate rate of movement, as in the case of the vigorous young executive as opposed to the equally vigorous young janitor. Rhythm also varies with the effect which one desires to create. Slow movement, for example, generally indicates formality and dignity, whereas faster movement indicates informality and ease. Let us note, however, that regardless of causes or eliciting circumstances, speed of movement can be judged as appropriate or inappropriate only in relation to the needs of those engaged in an interaction.

Distance

The distance which people establish among themselves when they interact is another important aspect of nonverbal communication in social life. Two observations on this subject have already been made. In the previous chapter, we discussed distance during communication as an important cross-cultural variable: members of different cultures communicate at different distances. We also advanced the suggestion earlier in this chapter that intimacy can be communicated in our culture through a composite of eye contact, facial expression, and distance. What, then, are the social uses of distance relationships?

A starting point for understanding man's use of space is provided by **ethology,** the study of animals in their natural habitats. **Ethologists** have discovered that most animals are equipped with a sense of both territoriality and flight distance. Animals establish dominance over a terrain from which they will drive away members of their own species. By dividing an area among themselves, the animals are allocating such vital resources as food and sex partners. Flight distance also has survival value, i.e., an animal will approach only so close to another species that he can escape from danger should the intruder prove hostile. Flight distances vary according to the fighting ability and speed of each species.

Human beings behave as if they too were territorial animals who establish specific distances between themselves and others. The mechanisms involved in human territoriality may not be the same as those of lower animals, but the overt activity is analogous. Robert Sommer delineates two meanings of space for human beings: as territory and as an area around the body.[9] Territory is defined as a stationary area, and the individual—the possessor of this area—will fight to maintain its visible boundaries. The meaning of territory might be difficult for members of other cultures to understand, but in the United States, where private property is revered, the concept is hardly novel. A family's home is its territory. Within the home, some rooms are the designated territories of the various family members. In like fashion, a streetcorner may be the shared territory of a group of adolescents, and a plush office may be the territory of an executive.

The area around the body, which Sommer calls **personal space,** is mobile—it moves with the body always at its center. The boundaries of personal space are invisible, and the individual will flee rather than fight if an intrusion is made into this space. Personal space can best be visualized as a "plastic bubble" which surrounds the individual. When people meet, they manipulate their bodies in such a way as to keep the walls of their bubbles intact. If one body pushes too close to the other, the bubbles bounce apart.

Territoriality is an important concept for understanding communication in our society. If we respect another's control over a specific area, each individual can control his own communication. Once we are in our own territory, we can exclude those with whom we do not wish to communicate. Without this kind of protection, each individual would become public property, available at all times to all comers. No one would be secure in preparing his performance, or in intimate communion with another to the exclusion of everyone else. Perhaps because of the centrality of territoriality to the ordering of social life, sanctions against the invasion of another's territory, at least in our society, are numerous and strong, ranging from laws against trespassing and searching without a warrant to phrases such as, "You could at least knock before entering."

Possession of territory is used to express status and dominance. As a rule, the greater an individual's prestige, the larger the territory he will control. This can be seen worked out in minute detail in the

[9] Robert Sommer, "Studies in Personal Space," **Sociometry,** XXII (1959), 247–60.

assignment of office space, wherein territorial allotments vary from the executive's relatively spacious office to the secretary's tiny cubicle. Quantity of space alone, however, does not necessarily establish the high prestige of possessing a given territory. Offices with windows or next to company presidents, may also signal importance.

Power to defend one's own territory and the right to invade that of others are also signs of dominance and prestige. To continue with the same example, the most important executive will control the area which is least accessible, sealed away from intruders by several doors and a handful of minions. The secretary will often be without the protection of a partition or a door, working in her tiny domain under the eyes of even casual visitors. This architectural arrangement reflects different prerogatives. For a subordinate to enter the boss' office without his consent would be a breach of etiquette, but it is expected that the boss will saunter into the realm of any subordinates without there being the slightest complaint.

The rigidity with which rules about territory are respected depends upon a host of factors. Among these factors, the immediate personal needs of the interactants are certainly important. If a person feels a strong need for protection from others, or a need to control a situation, he may well stress territorial rights. The type of relationship between communicators may also be important, for personal relationships require less formal observance of territorial boundaries than do business relationships.

The notion of personal space is manifested in human behavior by the observance of tacit rules about distancing. Sommer defines personal space as "the distance that the organism customarily places between itself and the other organisms." He has investigated regularities in personal distancing by a close study of the way in which individuals seat themselves in relation to one another. Few generalizations can be based on his results, but his work assists in greater understanding of the variables which influence man's use of space. For example, we now know that the significance of the simple distance between individuals must be qualified by the angle at which they are sitting. Since an individual tends to communicate more with a person sitting at right angles to him than with a person sitting by his side, we have some understanding of the tendency of people to sit at the corners of a table. Spacing tends to be influenced by the kind of communication—personal or impersonal—taking place: "The more personal the contact, the closer together people will sit." Environment can also be an influence, for the larger the room in which communication takes place, the closer individuals will sit to one another. Last, spatial arrangements may vary with the task set for the communicators. If the group is in a competitive situation, members tend to sit at a distance and opposite from one another, whereas members of groups that are cooperating prefer to sit at right angles.[10]

We must again stress the interdependence of various levels of nonverbal communciation in order to understand why human beings space themselves in certain ways. Seating in a group, for example, may be integrally related to visual cues. Sommer reports that competitors sit at opposite sides of a table so that they can watch one another closely. Similarly, Strodtbeck and Hook, examining spatial relationships in a simulated jury room, assert that seating position and visual cues determine who likes whom. Those persons who are seated in positions where they can inconspicuously watch one another express the greatest affiliation, because they can see each other's reactions.[11]

The study of personal distance has direct application in facilitating better communication. For example, from our study of proxemics we now know that the straight rows of chairs in classrooms prevent students from interacting with one another. Some educators have immediately seized upon this notion and recommended that all classrooms should be arranged with the chairs forming a circle. Unfortunately, in making this sort of recommendation, they have oversimplified what could be a very useful idea: people should be arranged to suit their communicative needs at any given moment, not to suit the janitor or to fit some abstract notion of good order or esthetics. Sommer suggests, for example, that

> at a school for disturbed children, it might be useful to have tables 2 feet by 4 feet. If the counselor wants the children to interact, he can place them so that they will be two feet from one another. If he wants to restrict their interaction, he can place them so that the table space between them will be four feet.[12]

[10] **Ibid.; idem,** "The Distance for Comfortable Conversation: A Further Study," **Sociometry,** XXV (1962), 111–16; **idem,** "Further Studies of Small Group Ecology," **Sociometry,** XXVIII (1965), 337–48.
[11] **Ibid.;** Fred L. Strodtbeck and L. Harmon Hook, "The Social Dimensions of a Twelve-Man Jury Table," **Sociometry,** XXIV (1961), 397–414.
[12] Robert Sommer, "Leadership and Group Geography," **Sociometry,** XXIV (1961), 109.

Thus, spatial arrangements should not be fixed without thought as to their future impact on human relationships.

Personal appearance and clothing

The types of nonverbal signals discussed so far involve immediate action. They fall under Ruesch and Kees's broad designation of "action language." However, not all nonverbal communication is composed of such signals. Ask yourself how you judge the personality and social class of new acquaintances. Are your judgments made solely on the basis of their actions? We suspect not. Certain relatively stable characteristics of personality and social position are most clearly projected through personal appearance and clothing.

The human body is perhaps the most basic element of "object language." Each of us probably has a conception of the relationship between body build and personality, which undoubtedly reflects some general stereotypes. The most precise statement of these stereotypes can be found in various systems of **somatotyping.** The most popular of these systems proposes three ideal types of physique: the muscular man or woman is a **mesomorph;** the person who is overweight and flabby is an **endomorph;** and the frail, thin person is an **ectomorph.** Naturally, no human being falls completely into any one of these three categories. Although a very strong man may be predominantly mesomorphic, he will also have endomorphic and ectomorphic characteristics.

In addition to describing physical types, systems of somatotyping attempt to assert a connection between physique and personality. A person who is predominantly ectomorphic is often described as timid, sensitive, and esthetic, the mesomorph is impulsive and strong-willed, and the endomorph is lethargic and lazy. Such characterizations probably are not valid in the sense that a physiological relationship between body type and mental processes exists. This is not to deny, however, that body type does affect communicative behavior.

Body type is a way of categorizing people which is often used in our society. Through our conditioning by the mass media, we have come to associate specific social roles with certain body types. The leading man in films is usually a mesomorph, the successful businessman is frequently stereotyped as an endomorph, and the seminarian, minister, or teacher is usually portrayed by an ectomorph. The media, of course, are only amplifying the conventional beliefs of society in general. By acting as though body type really does make a difference, we change our communicative behavior in order to give reality to categories which may have little inherent value. In the same way, the possessors of particular body types come to learn from the reactions of others that they should be assertive or shy or domineering.

The categorization of individuals on the basis of their personal appearance can, of course, border on the ludicrous. The blurb on the jacket of a recently published tome on facial appearance asserts that **"Knowledge of the language of the face** will equip you to be more successful in communicating with people—and influencing them." By "language of the face," the author means such fixed characteristics as a square-shape to the face, vertical creases between the eyebrows, and a medium-high, wide forehead. On the basis of such fixed features as these, the author infers hundreds of personality characteristics. One example will give the flavor of his inferences:

> When dealing with a fine textured skin person, remember:
>> He is very sensitive and easily offended.
>> He is inclined to be very formal.
>> He is very reserved and conventional.
>> He is soft spoken.[13]

Although such assertions have the scientific validity of an astrological forecast, they do tell us something about the way categorization can occur on the basis of physical appearance. If these generalizations were widely accepted, they would have tremendous impact on communicative behavior. We would then begin to treat all thin-skinned persons among us in special ways, and they would come to expect such treatment. The irony is, of course, that we all do use signs such as physical stature to determine how we should act toward other people.

Almost everyone makes some sort of effort to control his physical appearance in order to control the reactions of others. Weight-lifters, sunbathers, and dieters try to change their bodies. The rest of us try to wrap ourselves in cloth which will create an appearance to which others will react in a positive way. The way one dresses may be a response to deep-seated psychic intentions. One psychiatrist has written that:

[13] M. E. Mitchell, **How to Read the Language of the Face** (New York: The Macmillan Company, 1968), p. 17.

the way a woman dresses has intimate connections with the unconscious impression of herself which she wishes to convey, first to her
inner conscience, and later to the environment. This is a complex picture, based on **infantile repressed ideas of oneself, narcissistic identi-
fications** dating from early childhood, **inner defenses, guilt, compro-
mises, renunciations.**[14]

Although such psychoanalytic theory may help us to understand how
individuals dress, an approach which emphasizes the social function
of clothing may be better suited to understanding the sign value of
styles of dress. Barber and Lobel note that fashion is not socially irra-
tional: "It means several different things . . . and all its different
meanings are socially and culturally structured." They describe
fashion as an exercise in status display in which clothes are the signs
of their wearers' roles.[15] To extend their analysis somewhat, we can
say that clothes are sign-objects. To the wearer, they represent an
effort to control the reactions of others, and to the observer, they are
the means by which individuals can be socially classified.

Summary

In this chapter, we have reviewed some of the ways by which individuals communicate nonverbally in the United States. In indicating
that eye movement, facial expression, body movement, spatial relationships, and personal appearance and clothing all have expressive
significance, we do not pretend to have exhausted the list of meaningful cues in our society. Hopefully, however, we have indicated to
the reader how social relationships depend upon nonverbal communicative behavior.

---

[14] Edmund Bergler, **Fashion and the Unconscious** (New York: Brunner, 1953),
p. 138.
[15] Bernard Barber and Lyle S. Lobel, " 'Fashion' in Women's Clothes and the
American Social System," **Social Forces**, XXXI (1952), 124–31.

EIGHT

Exercises in nonverbal communication

Unapplied knowledge atrophies from disuse. You must test the ideas presented in the preceding chapters if they are to be a force in improving your communication. Nonverbal phenomena can be observed anywhere with a minimum of equipment, for the major prerequisite is merely that you have people with whom to work. Since this presents no great obstacle, nonverbal communication can be studied with extraordinary ease under the widest range of circumstances.

This chapter consists of exercises designed to isolate different kinds of nonverbal cues which usually occur together, as a mélange, in human interaction. The exercises should help simplify more complex activity in normal life. By using these exercises, the individual will become more aware of the different dimensions of communication.

These exercises are not psychological experiments, but simple explorations in communication. Unlike experiments, they do not attempt to rigidly control all the variables involved in obtaining the results. Consequently, you should be careful in generalizing your reactions to other people and situations. Nor should the exercises presented here be considered the only way nonverbal communication can be explored. The ultimate exercise in communication is finding for yourself new ways of discovering greater satisfaction for yourself and for others through human relationships.

Exercise I: stereophonic speaking

Purpose. This exercise attempts to determine the basis upon which an audience will focus on one speaker rather than another, if both are speaking at the same time. What holds the audience's attention: is it how the speaker delivers his message, the message itself, or how the speaker looks when he delivers his speech? Or perhaps a special combination of all three elements is responsible. This exercise is designed to examine these variables of public speaking.

Procedure.

Step I.   Two members of the group stand 8 to 10 feet in front of the audience, and 3 feet from one another.

Step II.   At a signal from the leader, the speakers begin to talk simultaneously on any topic they choose.

Step III. Speakers are restricted to an imaginary circle of 12 inches in diameter, and are encouraged to ignore their partners and keep talking at all costs.

Step IV. At a signal from the leader, speakers should stop and two new speakers be asked to replace them.

Step V.   After several pairs of speakers have performed, all members of the group should form one large circle for discussion.

Discussion. We have all had the experience of two people talking to us at the same time. We try desperately to be polite, giving each speaker a bit of attention to let him know we are listening. Here we have recreated such a dilemma, but with a purpose: to find out what each speaker will do to affect our attentional state. Some general questions may help you get started in analyzing what happened.

1. Which speaker monopolized your attention?
2. Did your attention shift from speaker to speaker?
3. Which speaker's message do you remember best?
4. Which speaker did you find more credible?
5. What do you think your reaction might have been had you not seen the speakers while they spoke?
6. Did you notice any kinesic cues which contributed to or detracted from the speeches?
7. Did either of the speakers become interested in his partner's speech

and thereby lose track of his own? Why do you think this sometimes happens?

Exercise II: what's in a name?

Purpose. How do people react to being arbitrarily labeled, and how do they respond to others who are similarly labeled? Everyone wears many labels, whether they are aware of this or not. These labels include how one acts, what clothes one wears, what possessions one has. All these labels are the basis of lasting impressions on others. This exercise should make you more aware of the dynamics and effects of the labeling process.

Procedure.

Step I.   Buy as many gum-backed labels as there are people involved in the exercise. Type on each label one of the following words:

cheapskate	pickpocket	coward
communist	ex-convict	hero
antisemite	troublemaker	genius
lover	hypochondriac	gossip
snob	neurotic	fool

Step II.   Line up the participants and affix labels to their foreheads. Do not allow people to see their own labels.

Step III. Instruct the group to move about the room, interacting freely with one another. Any nonverbal cues may be used, plus the naturally available props in the room. There is to be absolutely no talking or writing. Continue for 15 to 20 minutes.

Step IV. Form one large circle for discussion.

Discussion. Even though they know they are playing a game, participants seem to take this exercise very seriously. As in life, individuals begin to fulfill the role which the label assigns to them. In one group using this exercise, a girl wore the label "dental model." After a number of people passed her smiling, she began to smile at everyone who approached her. A friendly boy, labeled "ex-convict," began to behave hostilely to the group whose members were avoiding him. Each group will have somewhat different reactions to this experience. Here are some questions to begin the analysis of what happened in yours:

1. Before you knew what your label was, what was your attitude toward it?
2. How did you feel during this exercise?
3. At what point did you suspect the kind of label you were wearing? Explain.
4. Did you behave toward others according to the labels they bore?
5. Were any of the labels you saw incompatible with the people who were wearing them?
6. What are some of the unseen labels you think you wear in daily life? Explain how you know what they are.

Exercise III: nonverbal autobiography

Purpose. Nonverbal cues do not occur alone, but within a context. Often a cue that occurs in isolation is meaningless, but if it occurs in concert with certain other cues, it might have an important meaning. Consider a smile (retraction of the corners of the mouth) by itself. Now add to this smile a man who is 6 feet, 4 inches tall, eyes wide open and staring, both fists raised overhead ready to strike, a bit of froth seeping from the corners of his mouth. What is your judgment of the smile in this context?

In this exercise, observers are encouraged to notice as many things about a subject as possible and attempt to see relationships among them.

Procedure.

Step I. Everyone should be seated in a circle facing inward.

Step II. One member either volunteers or is selected to step to the center of the circle.

Step III. Once he is in the center, this member is invited to tell the group anything about himself **without using words.**

Step IV. After about 2 minutes, the person in the center returns to his seat and picks someone else to replace him.

Step V. After several people have gone to the center, the entire group should discuss what has happened and why.

Discussion. When you examine the behavior and feelings elicited by this experience, make sure you systematically discuss all the various types of nonverbal communication. Within the limits of tact, discuss what was communicated unintentionally as well as intentionally. Notice also how certain people in the group characteristically perceive some cues while they ignore others. Some further questions to consider include:

1. What was the most salient nonverbal cue you noticed?
2. Were the performers' movements purposeful?
3. Could you make any judgments about the performers' personalities from the clothes they wore, their movements, or their postural attitudes? Were these cues consistent with one another?
4. What cues gave you the best insight into the emotional state of each of the performers?

Exercise IV: dialogue in darkness

Purpose. Much nonverbal communication involves the sense of sight. We watch people move their faces, body, and hands, and we see their proxemic relation to us. We also speak with the expectation that others are watching us as well as listening to us. How does visual deprivation in normally sighted individuals affect the way they communicate? Will the ability to receive, integrate, and transmit information suffer as a result of lack of vision? This exercise is a simple probe of these questions.

Procedure.

Step I.   Arrange group members in clusters of 5 or 6, and seat them in circles.

Step II.   Choose a topic for discussion. Suggestions:
  a. Should a license be required for having children?
  b. The decline of the male image in the United States.
  c. The pros and cons of transexual surgery.
  d. Cryonics: mortality and morality.
  e. The ethics of polyandry.
  f. Does humor help or hinder in the classroom?

Step III. Have blindfolds placed on all participants.

Step IV.   Commence discussion of the chosen topic for 10 to 20 minutes.

Step V.   Stop the discussion and form one large circle for discussion.

Discussion. This exercise may be analyzed on several different levels, the most important of which is the personal level—how participants felt about themselves and about others during the experience. A second level for analysis is the effectiveness of the group in accomplishing its assigned task. The following questions may help you begin thinking about what happened:

1. How did you feel with the blindfold on? Explain.
2. Did your inability to see the people with whom you were talking interfere with your ability to concentrate?
3. Did you have any difficulty hearing what was said?
4. Do you think your sense of distance was affected?
5. Did you become aware of anything which you had not noticed before this experience?
6. Do you think you gestured more or less than you usually do?

Exercise V: acoustic dampening

Purpose. "I can't hear you. Wait till I put on my glasses." Because senses are in many ways interdependent, a lessening of the functional capacity of one sense may affect the others. Will a person's performance in group discussion be modified by artificially dampening his ability to hear? Will the effects be different for different individuals? These are several of the questions this exercise is designed to answer.

Procedure.

Step I. Arrange group members in clusters of 5 or 6, and seat them in a circle.

Step II. Give each person two sterile pieces of cotton to be placed one in each ear.

Step III. After cotton is distributed, choose a topic for discussion. Then have participants place the cotton in their ears.

Step IV. When the discussion has continued for 15 to 20 minutes, it should be halted and the cotton removed.

Step V. Form one large circle for discussion.

Discussion. Unless a person receives the conversational feedback to which he is accustomed, his communication pattern may change. He may communicate more or less, or in higher or lower amplitude—perhaps with louder talking, broader gestures, and the like. Consider the following questions:

1. What was your emotional response to this exercise?
2. Were you annoyed by those who perhaps could not hear you well enough?
3. Do you think the choice of topic could have any bearing upon the extent to which dampened hearing could be a significant liability?
4. Did you notice any change in the extent of eye contact in this exercise?

5. Was there any increase in physical contact, or in the physical relationship of the group members?

Exercise VI: open net/closed net

Purpose. This unit explores reactions to physical contact during group discussion. To examine these reactions, we have chosen a simple act—handholding. You will recall from Chapter 3 that attitudes toward various forms of physical contact are not uniform throughout the world. In Vietnam, for example, it is proper for men to hold hands in public, whereas such behavior in the United States is almost sure to evoke an indictment of homosexuality.

Procedure.

Step I.   Arrange group members in clusters of 5 or 6, and seat them in a circle.

Step II. A topic for discussion is assigned or agreed upon.

Step III. Discuss the topic for 8 to 12 minutes.

Step IV. Interrupt the discussion and instruct the participants to hold hands. Continue the discussion from the point at which it was broken off.

Step V.   After an additional 8 to 12 minutes, stop the discussion and form one large circle for discussion.

Discussion. Reactions to holding hands range from annoyance to distinct pleasure. In some individuals, this simple act elicits feelings of cohesion with the group, but others develop varying degrees of anxiety. Some of the variables which produce these reactions involve personality structure and feelings toward the group, situational factors such as the reaction of the people on either side of one, and the content of the discussion. It helps to begin analysis of this experience by discussing the effect of the topic on the previous discussion. If the subject under discussion was an intimate one, did the conversation become more upsetting when participants held hands? Or did the group, already knowing the purpose of the exercise, deliberately choose an impersonal topic? Other questions you might consider include:

1. Did you enjoy or resent this handholding exercise? Talk about the reasons for your reaction.
2. Did holding hands interfere in any way with your ability to think clearly?

3. Did holding the hand of a member of your own sex have any effect on you?
4. Did the person whose hand you held communicate nonverbally with you?

Exercise VII: touch and tell

Purpose. Think of your best friend's face and speculate on how well you could describe it to an artist so that he could draw an accurate sketch. Can you put into words how an ice cube feels so that someone who has never felt one could get a clear idea of what you were talking about? In this exercise we will test whether a person without special training can distinguish one face from another by touch alone. We will thus be able to see how external stimuli, sense receptors, and the central nervous system function together.

Procedure.

Step I.   One person who wishes to test his sense of touch is asked to come to the front of the room. He is then blindfolded.

Step II. Five or 6 people are then chosen and asked to sit in the front of the room, facing the person who will perform the exercise.

Step III. Each of the persons to be identified is touched about the face by the subject for one minute.

Step IV. When all subjects have been touched, one will be chosen to be resubmitted for identification. In the final phase, the person doing the touching must attempt to correctly identify the person he is touching solely on the basis of tactile memory.

Discussion. Most Americans, because they have been raised in a culture in which touching an acquaintance is generally forbidden, may not perceive tactile sensations with a high degree of discrimination. The ability to concentrate and remember may be further curtailed by these inhibitions against touching. Notice the cautious way most subjects go about their manual exploration of another's face. A discussion of this exercise might center on these questions:

1. What was your emotional attitude toward this exercise?
2. How did you feel as your face was being explored?
3. Do you think you would recognize your own face by touch if someone else were wearing it and you felt it?

4. Could you make any judgment about the person who was feeling your face by the way he felt it?

Exercise VIII: proxemics and the small group

Purpose. We have already discussed how the use of space can be a source of nonverbal communication. In this exercise, we will test the effects of various proxemic arrangements (see Figure 8–1).

Procedure.
Step I. Two groups of 6 persons are created. The first group is instructed to sit in a circle as close to one another as they can.

Figure 8–1. Arrangement of groups for Exercise VIII

The second group is also told to sit in a circle with their chairs two feet apart.

Step II. Each group is assigned a topic for a 20 minute discussion. The topic for group 1 (close distance) should be an impersonal subject of public policy. The topic for group 2 (far distance) should be a taboo subject of the type usually discussed among intimates.

Step III. Two new groups of 7 persons are formed. If you have enough people, this step may be taken simultaneously with Step I.

Step IV. In group 3, 6 participants may be seated in a conventionally arranged circle. The seventh is asked to stand in the middle of the circle. In group 4, 6 participants stand in a circle, and the seventh is asked to sit on the floor in the middle of the circle.

Step V. Once they are arranged, groups 3 and 4 can discuss any mutually agreeable subject.

Step VI. After all the exercises are finished, one large circle should be formed to discuss what took place.

Discussion. Where you sit, stand, or lie in relation to others is of real importance. Two dynamics essentially were in operation in these exercises: the variations in the amount of space between subjects on a horizontal plane (eye level) and on a vertical plane. Groups 1 and 2 were operating on the same plane, but at different levels of physical intimacy. Groups 3 and 4 had the same proximity, but the different vertical plane in which the seventh person in each was located may have caused real disturbance. Some questions about what happened include:

1. Did the members of the group who were discussing the taboo topic alter their proxemic relationships with one another?
2. Did the group discussing the less exciting topic alter its initial positioning?
3. How did you feel in your group?
4. In a great number of churches, the pulpit is located above the congregation so that the worshippers will have to look up. What is your opinion of this arrangement?
5. To what extent could you change the behavior of people in your home by deliberately arranging the furniture in some special way? Explain in detail.
6. What significance, if any, do you assign to the phrases, "I want someone to look up to," or, "He's always looking down on me."

Exercise IX: nonverbal communication through smell

Purpose. Man has a poorly developed sense of smell as compared to certain lower forms of animals. Men have greatly varying abilities to smell definitively. The Australian bushman, for example, depends upon his sense of smell for survival far more than the Madison Avenue executive. Although the ability to detect odors seems to play less and less of a role in modern living, some such ability is still necessary.

Procedure. This is the same as in Exercise VII, except that **smell** is to be substituted for touch.

Discussion. We can learn something merely from the reaction of certain people to the idea of this exercise. As with regard to their attitude toward touching, Americans feel hostile about smelling each other. They consider anyone who smells another person crass and vulgar. Stand in any crowded place in America and pretend to be smelling the person next to you. You will either be arrested or punched in the nose. Again, as with touch, this is not a universal attitude. In the Arab world, for example, standing close and breathing directly into someone's face is considered proper etiquette, whereas in the United States, it is considered rather gross.

There thus seem to be two culturally distinct attitudes toward smelling: some people are smell-oriented and some are nonsmell-oriented. The former smell everything, e.g., food, clothing, upholstery, lavatories, restaurants, and themselves. The latter make every effort to avoid anything that even hints of an odor. (Naturally, there are many people whose attitudes are between these two extremes.) In this exercise, watch carefully both the person doing the smelling and the person who is being smelled. Notice both kinesic and proxemic reactions to the act.

Recommended questions.
1. Why do you think you **failed** or **succeeded** in identifying someone by using your sense of smell? Explain.
2. Did you draw any conclusions about the persons you smelled in terms of their personality, character, or personal habits?
3. Did this exercise offend you? Explain.

4. How much of your own personal life depends upon your sense of smell? Explain.
5. If you were confronted with food that smelled bad but tasted good, would you eat it? Conversely, if food smelled good but tasted bad, would you eat it? Why?

Exercise X: international taste festival

Purpose. People in the various parts of the world display different attitudes toward food. One of the most dramatic indications of this is the variation in the time people take to eat a particular meal. In some countries a minimum of two hours is needed, whereas in others, 20 minutes seems adequate. The eating of food is indeed a source of nonverbal communication. Just how it communicates is the focus of this exercise. A group of people who are exposed to a table which is laden with delicious desserts from all over the world will be obliged, by the use of their senses, to tell as much about the country from which each dessert came as possible.

Procedure. Each member of the group is instructed in advance to bring in a dessert delicacy from some country in the world. There are to be no duplicates, and each dish should be labeled with its name and the country of origin.

Step I.   All desserts are placed in a row on a long table along with the necessary eating utensils.

Step II.   One at a time, each member approaches the table, picks up a utensil, and chooses a dessert.

Step III.   Based upon how the dessert looks, tastes, smells, and feels, the person who is eating should be able to make inferences about the characteristics of the country and the people of its origin.

Step IV.   One by one, each member is to go to the table and repeat the ritual.

Step V.   When this is finished, a large circle is formed and as many aspects of the experience as possible are to be discussed.

Discussion. The cliché, "some eat to live, while others live to eat," is a fairly reliable observation. Most of us fall into one of these categories. Have you ever used a restaurant as an **observatory?** Watching people eat is a thoroughly fascinating pastime, and very inexpensive.

Those who eat to live display a nonverbal stoicism barely capable of overcoming inertia. They rarely hurry or look at the food as it leaves the plate on its way to their mouths. The passionate eater who lives to eat, however, seldom takes his eyes off his food and moves it from plate to mouth with incredible speed and precision. In sum, people's attitudes toward food, nonverbally expressed can tell us a great deal about their personalities.

Exercise XI: proxemics: sociopedality on a one-to-one basis

Purpose. Another method of testing the effects of altered spatial relationships is by the use of one-to-one relationship. The object is to learn how people react to having friends, strangers, business associates, and loved ones walk, sit, or stand 6 to 8 inches closer than they normally do.

Procedure. The rules are simple. Those who are participating are told that during the course of any normal day, they should assume physical positions as close as possible to as many people as they can. Some of the more practical places to try this are in elevators, public transportation, school rooms, libraries, cafeterias, restaurants, homes, and offices. **A word of caution:** although most people will not react badly to such nearness, on occasion some people will become hostile. Therefore, we advise discretion wherever and whenever possible.

Earlier we learned that each of us is surrounded by an invisible bubble which we called our "personal bubble." Although the diameter of these circles of space vary according to time, place, and circumstance, they usually measure from 2 to 4 feet. Thus, we will be invading other people's bubbles without an invitation just to see what will happen.

Discussion. If properly done, this exercise should bring to light a number of very interesting phenomena, i.e., how people think, feel, and behave toward their personal space. Some of the determinants which can affect such behavior are: age, nationality, intelligence, personality, previous conditioning, time, place, physical appearance, and the relationship between the interacting parties.

Generally speaking, most people tend to back away when they are approached too closely. Strangely, if the approaching party is a female and her victim a male, he is more inclined to back away than another woman. Clichés such as, "don't talk to strangers," "keep your distance," and "know your place" are but a few examples of how behavioral norms pertaining to space are woven into our language. But, as we suggested in Chapter 6 on cross-cultural nonverbal codes, proxemic practices are not universally uniform. They differ not only from country to country, but from section to section within a country as well. One thing is apparent—spatial conventions are patterned and can be conservatively predicted in any culture.

Other things we should watch for when we confront people are **eye contact, diminished concentration levels,** and the **specific remarks people make.** For example, you will notice that the closer people are to one another, the less eye contact they maintain. Conversely, the farther apart they are, the more eye contact there is. Also, notice that certain individuals find it difficult to concentrate when someone stands too close to them. We recall the case of a college student who approached her teacher with a question, asking it with her face a scant four inches away from his. The teacher replied, "Would you mind moving back—I can't hear you." Drawing back only slightly, the student repeated her question. Obviously still disturbed, the teacher scurried behind his desk and ordered her to sit down. One additional type of verbal response to nearness may be statements such as, "Hey, what do you think you're doing?" or, "What's the matter with you?" Many of those who are approached will simply laugh, since they will not know what else to do. Psychologists tell us that this is a tension-reducing device.

Perhaps a few leading questions will help you get at additional meaningful material:

1. Is there a correlation between an individual's distancing practices and his personality?
2. What are some of the public situations in which people stand unusually close to each other?
3. Do audiences who are waiting to see an X-rated movie stand as close to one another as they do when they are waiting to see a G-rated film?
4. Do you think such things as **arguing distances, talking distances,** and **business distances** actually exist?
5. In standing close together, do you think it makes any difference if people stand face-to-face, back-to-back, back-to-side, side-to-side, or back-to-front?

Bibliography

For a more extended general overview of particular areas of nonverbal research, you should see:

Birdwhistell, Ray. **Kinesics and Context.** Philadelphia: University of Pennsylvania Press, 1970.

Hall, Edward. **Hidden Dimension.** Garden City, N.Y.: Doubleday & Company, Inc., 1966.

————. **Silent Language.** Garden City, N.Y.: Doubleday & Company, Inc., 1959.

Ruesch, Jurgen, and Weldon Kees. **Nonverbal Communication.** Berkeley: University of California Press, 1956.

Sommer, Robert. **Personal Space.** Englewood Cliffs, N.J.: Prentice-Hall, Inc., 1969.

The Birdwhistell volume contains an excellent bibliography. Two other easily accessible bibliographic sources are:

Barnlund, Dean. **Interpersonal Communication.** Boston: Houghton Mifflin Company, 1968, pp. 536–42.

Sebeok, Thomas, **et al. Approaches to Semiotics.** The Hague: Mouton, 1964, **passim.**

Besides the works cited in the text, valuable further reading will be found in:

123

Aiken, L. "The Relationship of Dress to Selected Measures of Personality in Undergraduate Women," **Journal of Social Psychology,** LIX (1963), 119–28.

Allport, G. W., and H. Cantril. "Judging Personality from Voice," **Journal of Social Psychology,** V (1934), 37–55.

Allport, G. W., and P. Vernon. **Studies in Expressive Movement.** New York: The Macmillan Company, 1933.

Asher, J. "The Learning Strategy of the Total Physical Response: A Review," **Modern Language Journal,** L (1966), 79–84.

Barbara, D. A. "The Value of Nonverbal Communication in Personality Understanding," **Journal of Nervous and Mental Diseases,** CXXIII (1956), 286–91.

Beier, E., and J. Stumpf. "Cues Influencing Judgment of Personality Characteristics," **Journal of Consulting Psychology,** XXIII (1959), 219–25.

Berger, M. M. "Nonverbal Communication in Group Psychotherapy," **International Journal of Psychotherapy,** VIII (1958), 161–78.

Birdwhistell, R. L. "Paralanguage 25 Years after Sapir," in H. W. Brosin, ed., **Lectures on Experimental Psychiatry.** Pittsburgh: University of Pittsburgh Press, 1961, pp. 43–63.

Birren, Faber. **Functional Color.** New York: Crimson Press, 1937.

Black, J. W. "The Effect of Room Characteristics upon Vocal Intensity and Rate," **Journal of the Acoustical Society of America,** XXII (1950), 174–76.

Bogardus, E. S. **Social Distance.** Yellow Springs, Ohio: Antioch Press, 1959.

Carpenter, C. R. "Territoriality: A Review of Concepts and Problems," in A. Roe and G. G. Simpson, eds., **Behavior and Evolution.** New Haven: Yale University Press, 1958.

Cline, M. G. "The Influence of Social Context on the Perception of Faces," **Journal of Personality,** XXV (1956), 142–58.

Cohen, A., and J. Starkweather. "Vocal Cues to Language Identification," **American Journal of Psychology,** LXXIV (1961), 90–93.

Compton, N. "Personal Attributes of Color and Design Preferences in Clothing Fabrics," **Journal of Psychology,** LIV (1962), 191–95.

Corbin, E. "Muscle Action as Nonverbal and Preverbal Communication," **Psychoanalytic Quarterly,** XXXI (1962), 351–63.

Crichtley, M. **The Language of Gesture.** London: Arnold, 1939.

Diebold, A. R., Jr. "Anthropological Perspectives: Anthropology and the Comparative Psychology of Communicative Behavior," in T. A. Sebeok, ed., **Animal Communication.** Bloomington: Indiana University Press, 1968, pp. 525–60.

Dittman, A. T., M. B. Parloff, and D. S. Boomer. "Facial and Bodily Expression: A Study of Receptivity of Emotional Cues," **Psychiatry,** XXVIII (1965), 239–44.

Efran, J., and A. Broughton. "Effect of Expectancies for Social Approval on Visual Behavior," **Journal of Personality and Social Psychology,** IV (1966), 103–7.

Ekman, P. "Body Position, Facial Expression and Verbal Behavior During Interviews," **Journal of Abnormal and Social Psychology,** LXVIII (1964), 295–301.

———. "Communication through Nonverbal Behavior: A Source of Information about an Interpersonal Relationship," in S. S. Tomkins and C. E. Izard, eds., **Affect, Cognition and Personality.** New York: Springer Press, 1965, pp. 390–442.

———. "Differential Communication of Affect by Head and Body Cues," **Journal of Personality and Social Psychology,** II (1965), 726–35.

———, and W. V. Friesen. "Nonverbal Leakage and Clues to Deception," **Psychiatry,** XXXII (1969), 88–106.

———, E. R. Sorenson, and W. V. Friesen. "Pan-cultural Elements in Facial Displays of Emotion," **Science,** CLXIV (1969), 86–88.

Feldman, Sandor. **Mannerisms of Speech and Gesture.** New York: International Universities Press, 1959.

Flugel, J. **The Psychology of Clothes.** London: Hogarth Press, 1930.

Frijda, N. H. "Facial Expression and Situational Cues," **Journal of Abnormal and Social Psychology,** LVII (1958), 149–53.

———. "Recognition of Emotion," in L. Berkowitz, ed., **Advances in Experimental Social Psychology,** Vol. IV. New York: Academic Press, 1969, pp. 167–223.

Frois-Whittmann, J. "The Judgment of Facial Expression," **Journal of Experimental Psychology,** XIII (1930), 113–51.

Gibson, J. J. "Observations on Active Touch," **Psychological Review,** LXIX (1962), 477–91.

Giedt, F. "Comparison of Visual, Content and Auditory Cues in Interviewing," **Journal of Consulting Psychology,** XIX (1955), 407–16.

Goffman, E. "Symbols of Class Status," **British Journal of Sociology,** II (1951), 294–304.

Haggard, E. A., and F. S. Isaacs. "Micromomentary Facial Expressions as Indicators of Ego Mechanisms in Psychotherapy," in L. A. Gottschalk and A. H. Averback, eds., **Methods of Research in Psychotherapy.** New York: Appleton-Century-Crofts, 1966.

Hall, E. "Proxemics," **Current Anthropology,** IX (1968), 84–107.

Harrison, P. "Non-Verbal Communication: Explorations into Time, Space, Action, and Object," in J. H. Campbell and H. W. Helper, eds., **Dimensions in Communication.** Belmont, Calif.: Wadsworth, 1965, pp. 158–74.

Hayes, F. "Gestures: A Working Bibliography," **Southern Folklore Quarterly,** XXI (1957), 218–317.

Hearn, G. "Leadership and the Spatial Factor in Small Groups," **Journal of Abnormal and Social Psychology,** LIV (1957), 269–72.

Hess, E. H. "Attitude and Pupil Size," **Scientific American,** CCXII (April 1965), 46–54.

Hoult, R. "Experimental Measurement of Clothing as a Factor in Some Social Ratings of Selected American Men," **American Sociological Review,** XIX (1954), 324–28.

Kanfer, F. "Verbal Rate, Eyeblink and Content in Structured Psychiatric Interviews," **Journal of Abnormal and Social Psychology,** LXI (1960), 341–47.

Kleck, R. "Physical Stigma and Nonverbal Cues Emitted in Face-to-Face Interaction," **Human Relations,** XXI (1968), 19–28.

Knapp, P. H., ed. **Expression of Emotion in Man.** New York: International Universities Press, 1963.

Kramer, E. "The Judgment of Personal Characteristics and Emotions from Nonverbal Properties of Speech," **Psychological Bulletin,** LX (1963), 408–20.

————. "Personality Stereotypes in Voice: A Reconsideration of the Data," **Journal of Social Psychology,** LXII (1964), 247–51.

Little, K. B. "Personal Space," **Journal of Experimental Social Psychology,** I (1965), 237–47.

Max, L. W. "Experimental Study of Motor Theory of Consciousness," **Journal of Comparative Psychology,** XXIV (1937), 310–44.

Mehrabian, A. "Orientation Behaviors and Nonverbal Attitude Communication," **Journal of Communication,** XVII (1967), 324–32.

————. "Relationship of Attitude to Seated Posture, Orientation and Distance," **Journal of Personality and Social Psychology,** X (1968), 26–30.

Montagu, M. F. A. "Natural Selection and the Origin and Evolution of Weeping in Man," **Science,** CXXX (1959), 1572–73.

Munn, N. L. "The Effect of Knowledge of the Situation upon Judgment of Emotion from Facial Expressions," **Journal of Abnormal Social Psychology,** XXXV (1940), 324–38.

Osgood, C. E. "Dimensionality of the Semantic Space for Communication via Facial Expressions," **Scandinavian Journal of Psychology,** VII (1966), 1–30.

Pierce, D. H., and J. D. Weinland. "The Effect of Color on Workmen," **Journal of Personality,** XIII (1934), 34–38.

Pittenger, R. E. "Linguistic Analysis of Tone of Voice in the Communication of Affect," **Psychiatric Research Reports,** VIII (1958), 41–54.

Pressey, S. L. "The Influence of Color upon Mental and Motor Efficiency," **American Journal of Psychology,** XXXII (1921), 326–56.

Reece, M., and R. Whitman. "Expressive Movements, Warmth, and Verbal Reinforcement," **Journal of Abnormal and Social Psychology,** LXIV (1962), 234–36.

Sainsbury, P. "Gestural Movement During Psychiatric Interview," **Psychosomatic Medicine,** XVII (1955), 458–69.

Scheflen, A. E. "The Significance of Posture in Communication Systems," **Psychiatry,** XXVII (1964), 316–33.

Scott, Ian, ed. **The Luscher Color Test.** New York: Random House, Inc., 1969, pp. 9–30, 51–71.

Sebeok, T. A. "Animal Communication," **International Social Science Journal,** XIX (1967), 88–95.

Secord, P., **et al.** "Personalities in Faces," **Genetic Psychology Monographs,** XLIX (1954), 231–79.

Sherrington, C. **The Integrative Action of the Nervous System.** New Haven: Yale University Press, 1961.

Simmel, G. "Sociology of the Senses: Visual Interaction," in R. E. Park and E. W. Burgess, eds., **Introduction to the Science of Sociology.** Chicago: University of Chicago Press, 1921.

Sommer, R. "Social Interaction on a Geriatrics Ward," **International Journal of Social Psychiatry,** IV (1958), 128–33.

———. "Sociofugal Space," **American Journal of Sociology,** LXXII (1967), 654–60.

Soskin, W. F., and P. E. Kauffman. "Judgment of Emotion in Word-Free Voice Samples," **Journal of Communication,** XI (1961), 73–80.

Starkweather, J. A. "Vocal Communication of Personality and Human Feelings," **Journal of Communication,** XI (1961), 63–72.

Steinzor, R. "The Spatial Factor in Face-to-Face Discussion Groups," **Journal of Abnormal and Social Psychology,** XLV (1950), 552–55.

Talmadge, M. "Expressive Graphic Movements and Their Relationship to Temperament Factors," **Psychological Monographs,** LXXII (1958), 1–30.

Thompson, D. F., and L. Meltzer. "Communication of Emotional Intent by Facial Expression," **Journal of Abnormal and Social Psychology,** LXVIII (1964), 129–35.

Thornton, G. "The Effect of Wearing Glasses upon Judgments of Personality Traits of Persons Seen Briefly," **Journal of Applied Psychology,** XXVIII (1944), 203–7.

Trager, C. L. "Paralanguage: A First Approximation," **Studies in Linguistics,** XIII (1958), 1–12.

Triandis, H. "Cognitive Similarity and Communication in a Dyad," **Human Relations,** XIII (1960), 279–87.

Vinacke, W. "The Judgment of Facial Expressions by Three National-Race Groups in Hawaii," **Journal of Personality,** XVII (1949), 407–29.

Wallis, W. A. "The Influence of Color on Apparent Size," **Journal of General Psychology,** XIII (1935), 193–99.

Warr, P. B. "Proximity as a Determinant of Positive and Negative Sociometric Choice," **British Journal of Social and Clinical Psychology,** IV (1965), 104–9.

Watzlawick, P., J. H. Beavin, and D. D. Jackson. **Pragmatics of Human Communication.** New York: W. W. Norton Company, Inc., 1967.

Wells, W. D., and B. Siegel. "Stereotyped Somatotypes," **Psychological Reports,** VIII (1961), 77–78.

Winick, C., and H. Holt. "Seating Position as Nonverbal Communication in Group Analysis," **Psychiatry,** XXIV (1961), 171–82.

Wolff, W. "Involuntary Self-Expression in Gait and Other Movements: An Experimental Study," **Character and Personality,** II (1933), 327–44.

Index

Action language, 9, 17, 105
  defined, 23
Adaptors, 25, 27
Affect displays, 25, 26–27
Argyle, Michael, 64, 66, 72, 93, 94–95
Asch, S. E., 6

Barber, Bernard, 107
Barker, Larry, 55–56
Barnlund, Dean, 16
Becker, Ernest, 67
Behavioral patterns, American
  distance, 101–105
  eye movement, 92–95
  facial expression, 95–97
  personal appearance and cloth-
    ing, 105–107
  posture, 98–99
Behaviorism, 48–49
Bergler, Edmund, 107
Birdwhistell, Ray, 18, 19, 27–28, 39,
    77, 83–84
Boas, Franz, 78
Body, the, as message medium, 47–
    51

Body communication, types of, 25–
    29
Body image boundary, 88–89
"Body language," 20, 33
Body movements, 25–26, 33–34
Body types, 105–106

Caillière, Maréchal de, 7
chemoceptors, 51–52
Coleman, J. C., 38
Communication
  defined, 18
  nonverbal. See Nonverbal com-
    munication
  verbal, 19–20, 20–22
Coping behavior, 31
Cultural differences
  in autonomic movements, 77
  in dance movements, 81–83
  among ethnic groups in the
    United States, 89–90
  in gestures, 76–77
  in movement communication, 80–
    85
  in postural communication, 78–80

Cultural differences—*Cont.*
  in proxemic communication, 85–88
  in ways of calling a waiter, 76–77
  in ways of pointing, 76
Culture
  differences in. **See** Cultural differences
  influence on communication behavior, 51, 52
  nonverbal ethnocentrism, 75–77
  source of differences in discrimination, 56
  source of meaning of nonverbal signs, 41–42

Darwin, Charles, 40–41
Dean, Janet, 93, 94–95
Deutsch, Felix, 45
DeVito, Joseph, 21
Discrimination between stimuli, 56–57
Distance, 52, 101–105. **See also** Proxemics
  personal space, 102, 103–105
  territory, 102–103
Dominance, expressed by possession of territory, 102–103

Ectomorphs, 105
Efron, David, 89–90
Ekman, Paul, 25–27, 35, 37, 42, 67–68, 96
Ellsworth, Phoebe, 37, 42, 68, 96
Emblems, 25–26
Emotion
  facial expression of, 36–40
  masking of, 97
  vocal expressions of, 35–36, 39–40
Endomorphs, 105
Ethnicity and tolerance, 89–90
Ethnocentrism, 75–77
Ethology, 101
Evans, Rowland, 7
Exline, Ralph, 93–94
Expressive behavior, 31
Eye movement, 92–95

Facial expression, 67–68, 95–97
  evolutionary explanation of, 40–41
  judgment of, 36–40
Facial expressions, universal, 42
Fast, Julius, 66
Fearing, Franklin, 30–31
Feedback, 15, 17–18, 54
Feldman, S. S., 45
Fisher, Seymour, 88
Forsten, Robert, 90
Friesen, Wallace, 25–27, 34, 35, 37, 42, 68, 96
Functions of nonverbal communication. **See** Social functions of nonverbal communication

Gans, Herbert, 89
Geldard, Frank A., 53
Gestures, 35, 99–101
  as regressive behavior, 45
Gibson, James, 93
Glazer, Nathan, 89
Goffman, Erving, 67, 69, 71
Gray, David, 93

Habit patterns, learning of, 60
Hall, Edward, 28, 51, 85–88, 89
Hastorf, Albert, 65
Hayes, Alfred S., 78
Herring, E., 54
Hewes, Gordon, 78, 79, 80
Hook, L. Harmon, 104
Hyperkinetic people, 101
Hypokinetic people, 101

Identity, social, 66–68. **See also** Social roles
Illustrators, 25, 26, 35
Individual differences
  in expressing and judging emotions, 36
  in perception of nonverbal signs, 16–18, 30
Innate traits, influence of on communication behavior, 51
Interoceptors, 53–54
Intrapersonal communication, 59–60

James, W., 98
Johnson, Lyndon B., 7–8
Jones, Stanley, 90
Judgment studies, 37–39

Kees, Weldon, 22–23, 25, 31, 105
Kinemorphs, 39
Kines, 39
Kinesics, 27–28, 39, 43
  defined, 28

Laban, Rudolf, 85
La Barre, Weston, 43
Landis, Carney, 37–38
Language
  acquisition of, 42
  symbols of, 21
Language ethnocentrism, 75–78
Larson, Charles, 90
Lasswell, Harold, 12
Levitt, Eugene, 40
Lie detectors, 59–60
Lip-synched movies, 83
Lobel, Lyle S., 107
Lomax, Alan, 80–82

MacLean, Paul, 59
Mahl, George, 24
Mahrabian, Albert, 19
Mead, Margaret, 76
Mental processes in nonverbal com-
    munication, 54–60
  discrimination, 56–57
  ideation, 58
  incubation, 58
  life orientation, 58
  regrouping of stimuli, 57
  symbol decoding, 57–58
  symbol encoding and transmis-
      sion, 59–60
Mesomorphs, 105
Messages. **See also** Nonverbal mes-
    sages
  body, the, as medium of, 47–51
  conflicting, 14
  nonverbal, distinguished from ver-
      bal, 20–22

Messages—*Cont.*
  simultaneous transmission of, 12
  verbal. **See** Verbal messages
Microkinesics, 28, 39
Mitchell, M. E., 106
Moynihan, Daniel, 89
Munari, Bruno, 33
Myokinetic rhythm, 100–101

Nature-nurture controversy on fa-
    cial expressions, 40–46
Needles, William, 45
Nonverbal communication
  defined, 20
  distinguished from verbal com-
      munication, 20–22
  intrapersonal, 59–60
  issues in defining, 29–32
  and mental processes. **See** Men-
      tal processes in nonverbal
      communication
  patterns in, 21
  social functions of. **See** Social
      functions of nonverbal com-
      munication
  and social identity, 66–68
  types of, 22–29
Nonverbal messages
  distinguished from verbal mes-
      sages, 20–22
  functions of, 35
  shaped by physiology, 52
Nonverbal signs
  individual differences in percep-
      tion of, 16–18, 30
  origins of, 40–46
    attitude theory, 44–45
    cultural explanation of, 41–42
    evolutionary explanation of, 40–
        41, 42–43
    psychoanalytic theory of, 45–46
  pancultural, 42
Nonverbal vocalizations, 23–24
Novak, Robert, 7

Object language, 105
  defined, 23

Ostwald, Peter, 47, 60

Paralanguage, 23–25
Parkinson, C. Northcote, 9
Pattie, James, 76
Perception, 16–18
  defined, 16
  of nonverbal signs, individual dif-
    ferences in, 16–18, 30
Personal space, 102, 103–105
Phillips, Gerald, 90
Physiological psychology, 48–50
Physiology of communication, 47–61
  neural impulses, 54–55
  stimulus reception, 51–54
  symbol encoding and transmis-
    sion, 59–61
Pick, Anne, 93
Postural communication, 78–80
Prekinesics, 27
Pressure receptors, 52
Property management, 29
Proprioceptors, 53
Proxemic communication, cultural
    differences in, 85–88
Proxemic patterns, affected by
    sense organs, 52
Proxemics, 28–29. See also Distance
Pseudo-affective behavior, 5
Psychoanalytic theory of expres-
    sion, 45–46
Psychology, behaviorist and physio-
    logical, 48–50

Regrouping of stimuli, 57
Regulators, 25, 26, 35
Roles, social. See Social roles
Rolf, Ida, 60
Ruesch, Jurgen, 21–22, 22–23, 25, 31,
    55, 105

Schuette, Dorothy, 93
Schulze, Gene, 24
Secord, Paul, 58
self-adaptors, 27
self-control, 68–72

self-feedback, 54
self-presentation, 66–68. See also
    Social roles
  and motor coordination, 72–73
Self-protection through self-control,
    68–72
Semantics, 17
Sense organs, 51–53
Sensory impressions, reception of,
    51–54
Signals
  for calling a waiter, 76–77
  partial inability to receive, 53
  personal appearance and cloth-
    ing, 105–107
Sign language, defined, 23
Signs, 34–35. See also Nonverbal
    signs
Social categories, 65–66, 71
Social functions of nonverbal com-
    munication, 62–74
  identity, maintenance of, 66–68
  integration of action and feelings,
    64–66
  role performance, 68–73
  transmission of information, 62–
    64
Social identity, 66–68. See also So-
    cial roles
Social kinesics, 28
Social roles, 68–73
  associated with body type, 105–
    106
  clothes as signs of, 107
Somatotypes, 105–106
Sommer, Robert, 102, 104
Sperry, R. W., 48, 55
Status, expressed by possession of
    territory, 102–103
Stimuli
  discrimination between, 56–57
  initiating, 14, 17
  physiology of reception of, 51–54
  regrouping of, 57
  screened by receptor end-organs,
    52–53
Stone, Gregory P., 88

Strauss, Anselm, 62–63
Strodtbeck, Fred L., 104
Sundene, Barbara, 40
Symbols
  decoding of, 57–58
  defined, 34
  of language, 21

Territoriality, 101–103
Thermoreceptors, 52
Tolerance of ethnic differences, 89–
  90

Verbal communication, 19–20
  distinguished from nonverbal
    communication, 20–22
Verbal messages
  emotional connotations of, 35–36

Verbal messages—*Cont.*
  relation to nonverbal messages,
    35
Vocal characterizers, 24
Vocal expression, judgment of, 35–
  36, 39–40
Vocal expressions of emotion, 35–36,
  39–40
Vocalizations, nonverbal, 23–24, 35
Vocal qualifiers, 24
Vocal segregates, 24
Voice set, 23–24, 35

Whiffen, T., 85
Williams, Frederick, 40
Wiseman, Gordon, 55–56
Wooldridge, Dean, 59

Zubeck, John, 54